SHELF LIFE

SHELF LIFE

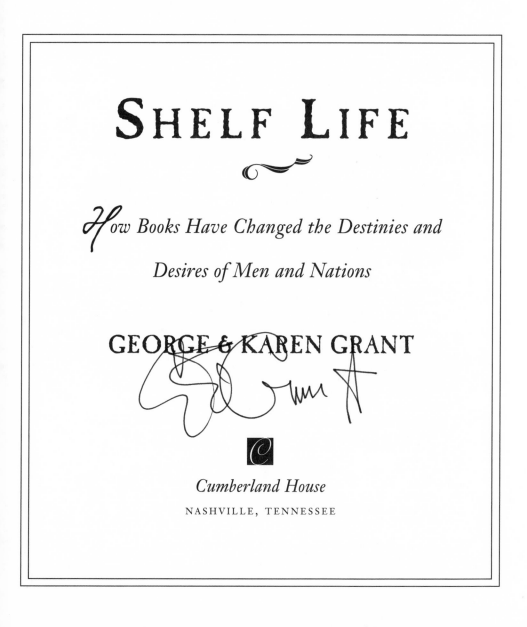

How Books Have Changed the Destinies and

Desires of Men and Nations

GEORGE & KAREN GRANT

Cumberland House

NASHVILLE, TENNESSEE

Jacket design by Tonya Presley
Text design by Bruce Gore, Gore Studios, Inc.

Library of Congress Cataloging-in-Publication Data

Grant, George, 1954-
  Shelf life : how books have changed the destinies and desires of men and nations /
  George & Karen Grant.
      p. cm.
    ISBN 1-58182-043-7 (pbk. : alk. paper)
    1. Books and reading. 2. Books and reading--Quotations, maxims, etc.
I. Grant, Karen B., 1955- II. Title.
Z1003 .G76 1999
028'.9--dc21

                                                            99-053169

Printed in the United States of America
1 2 3 4 5 6 7 8 9 — 03 02 01 00 99

To Aidan Mackey

CONTENTS

ACKNOWLEDGMENTS

"It is an old and healthy tradition that each home where the light of god-liness shone should have its own bookshelf. Blessed is the man or woman who has inherited such a cultural and spiritual bequest."
JOHN MACLEOD (1872–1948)

We have been blessed. We are the heritors of a remarkable cultural and spiritual bequest. We have enjoyed the old and healthy tradition of having our own bookshelf—indeed, our home is dominated with bookshelves and the books that fill them.

Over the years a number of family members and dear friends have richly contributed to that legacy. They have blessed us with encouragement, wise counsel, comfort, companionship, and, of course, books. They have always been, and always will be, an integral and essential aspect of our shelf life.

Our fellow laborers Greg and Sophia Wilbur, Hugh and Lisa Harris, Jim and Gwen Smith, Gene and Susan Hunt, Stephen and Tricia Mansfield, Robert and Kim Fulcher, Dan and Paige Pitts, Steve and Eve Marks, Randy and Lori Thomas, Duane and Kathy Ward, and Anthony and Sharon Gordon have been a constant support to us. Our prayer partners Tom and Jody Clark, Steve and Nancy Dragoo, Terry and Patty Gensemer, and Bill and Dawn Ruff have upheld us in good times and bad. Caren Covington, Jackie Lusk, and Chuck Wagoner organized our lives and kept the wolves from the door. Our yokefellows in the Empty Hands Fellowship, the Micah Class, and the Knox House program enriched our lives immeasurably. And our students at Bannockburn College, Gileskirk School, and Franklin Classical School make all our wide-ranging and often disparate efforts worthwhile, constantly reminding us of the things that matter most.

Aidan Mackey, director of the G. K. Chesterton Study Center at Oxford University, has long been a dear friend, a guide to literary England and Scotland, and a provocation to everything virtuous in the shelf life. He is responsible, perhaps more than any other individual, for our encouraging Chestertonian appetites and enlightening our bibliophilic dispositions. In the good providence of God, his example of keen scholarship, Christian charity, good humor, tender mercy, unfettered enthusiasm, vibrant energy, and warm hospitality has shaped our lives, sharpened our minds, and enriched our souls.

The good folks at Cumberland House, and particularly our dear friends Ron and Julia Pitkin, embraced our vision for books that were distinctly practical, down-to-earth, fun, historically informed, nondidactic, and yet fully within the parameters of a

Christian worldview. Their commitment to this series of books—as yet nameless, difficult to describe, and even more difficult to sell—has been a tremendous encouragement to us.

To all these, we offer our sincerest thanks.

The soundtrack for this project included works by Richard Searles, Barry and Shelly Phillips, Wes King, Steve Green, and Michael Card. Likewise, the midnight musings were provided by Thomas Chalmers, Arthur Quiller-Couch, C. S. Lewis, J. R. R. Tolkien, and Leland Ryken. Their influence, we hope, is obvious in both content and form.

Finally, it is our sincerest prayer that the blessing of the shelf life we have shared might be the means by which the light of godliness shines into the lives of our children, Joel, Joanna, and Jesse—that they may fully enjoy their cultural and spiritual bequest and thus know the breadth, depth, width, and height of grace.

Summer 1999
King's Meadow

INTRODUCTION

~

"Just as art needs no justification—we may rest assured that beauty, goodness, and truth are well able to fend for themselves—so also the shelf life needs no defense. Mere affirmation affords stark contrast enough with the howling wasteland of modern bohemianism."

TRISTAN GYLBERD (1954–)

This book is a celebration of the literate. It is a revelry of reading. It is an expression of joy in the blessing of books, stories, poems, sagas, legends, and all the things that literature seems to invoke or provoke in our lives.

It is not a protest. It is not a caveat. It is not an attempt at social analysis, criticism, or churlishness. Such an analysis is tempting. After all, literary affections have become increasingly rare and peculiar in our postmodern culture. People committed to a life of quiet reflection, of substantive thought, and to the inculcation of beauty, goodness, and truth have become a distinct minority.

According to author Richard Hoggart, we now live in a "post-literate society." It is an opinion shared by many. As a result, it has become commonplace for prognosticators of the future to herald the impending demise of literature, of books, indeed, of the printed word.

Such dire warnings are not unwarranted. There can be little doubt: Electronic mass media have become the dominant means of conveying and purveying modern culture today. Television is America's drug of choice—a kind of electronic valium. And virtually everyone across this vast land is using it. More than 98 percent of all households have at least one television set. In fact, more American households have television sets than have indoor plumbing. American preschoolers watch an average of more than twenty-seven hours of programming each week—more than four hours per day. On school nights American teens are limited to only about three hours of television viewing a night. In contrast, though, they spend about fifty-four minutes on homework, less than sixteen minutes reading, about fourteen minutes alone with their mothers, and less than five minutes with their fathers.

The average American child watches eight thousand made-for-television murders and a hundred thousand acts of violence before they get to junior high school. By the time the child has graduated from high school, that number will have doubled. The casual carnage is woven into supposedly real-life situations with amazing alacrity. One survey found that situation comedies, cartoons, and family dramas are just as likely to feature violence as police procedurals, medical dramas, and period masques.

This awful barrage is nothing new. While programming has certainly gotten more explicit, more brazen, and more perverse in recent years, television has always been a bastion of mindless barbarism. As early as 1961, Newton Minow, then the chairman of the Federal Communications Commission, assessed television in a scathing critique: "When television is bad, there is nothing worse. I invite you to sit down in front of your television set when your station goes on the air and stay there without a book, magazine, newspaper, profit-and-loss sheet, or rating book to distract you—and keep your eyes glued to that set until the station signs off. I can assure you that you will observe a vast wasteland. You will see a procession of game shows, violence, audience-participation shows, formula comedies about totally unbelievable families, blood and thunder, mayhem, violence, sadism, murder, western badmen, western good men, private eyes, gangsters, more violence, and cartoons. And endlessly, commercials—many screaming, cajoling, and offending. And most of all boredom. True, you will see a few things you will enjoy. But they will be very, very few. And if you think I exaggerate, try it."

Television is only the half of it. Americans see an average of sixty-seven full-length feature films per year—either in theaters or on video—an average of more than one each week. On average they own forty-two musical compact disks, sixteen video-game cartridges, and seven computer games. More than 35 percent of all American children have their own television sets; more than 80 percent own radios; almost 76 percent possess cassette or compact disk players; and while only 39 percent own personal computers, more than 68 percent have access to the Internet.

As Robert Bork has asserted, "Popular entertainment sells sex, pornography, violence, vulgarity, attacks on traditional forms of authority and outright perversion more copiously and more insistently than ever before in our history. It is no answer to point out that much of popular culture is harmless or even benign. The culture has changed, is changing, and the change is for the worse. The worst is the leading edge."

Setting aside for a moment any analysis of the entertainment being consumed by Americans, just the fact that they are soaking up so much sheer mediamorphic entertainment is profoundly unsettling. With such a barrage of sights and sounds, there can hardly be any time, money, or inclination left for reading books.

According to Neil Postman in his must-read manifesto, *Amusing Ourselves to Death*, there are two means by which the spirit of a great culture may be undermined—one is portrayed in George Orwell's horrifying novel of oppression, *1984*; the other is described in Aldous Huxley's equally horrifying novel of debauchery, *Brave New World*. "In the first—the Orwellian—culture becomes a prison," Postman argued. "In the second—the Huxleyan—culture becomes a burlesque." Clearly, in America, Orwell's prophecies are of small relevance, but Huxley's are well underway toward being realized. After all, as Postman has all too obviously pointed out: "America is engaged in the world's most ambitious experiment to accommodate itself to the technological distractions made possible by the electric plug. This is an experiment that began slowly and modestly in the mid-nineteenth century and has now, in the latter half of the twentieth, reached a perverse maturity in America's consuming love affair with mass media. As nowhere else in the world, Americans have moved far and fast in bringing to a close the age of the slow-moving printed word and have granted to the media sovereignty over all their institutions. By ushering in the age of television, America has given the world the clearest available glimpse of the Huxleyan future."

Essentially, Orwell feared that we would become a society where books would be banned. But what Huxley feared was that there would be no reason to ban a book, because no one would want to read one. According to Postman, "Orwell feared those who would deprive us of information. Huxley feared those who would give us so much that we would be reduced to passivity and egoism. Orwell feared that the truth would be concealed from us. Huxley feared the truth would be drowned in a sea of irrelevance. Orwell feared we would become a captive culture. Huxley feared we would become a trivial culture, preoccupied with some equivalent of the feelies, the orgy porgy, and the centrifugal bumblepuppy." In *1984*, people are controlled by the infliction of pain. In *Brave New World*, they are controlled by the infliction of pleasure. In short, Orwell feared that what we hate will ruin us: Huxley feared that what we love will ruin us. We must face the very real possibility that Huxley, not Orwell, was right. We have actually begun the process of "amusing ourselves to death."

In times like these, a resolute shelf life might seem to be altogether archaic, antiquarian, and awkward. Serious reading is simply not in vogue—long ago it was left in the dust bin of history by the newfangled, gee-whiz gadgetry of industrial contemporaniety and progressive modernity.

All this is all the more reason for this book—all the more reason for the celebration of the civilized culture that grows up around the printed word in all its multifarious manifestations. Each chapter profiles a particular aspect of this lost cause of the literary life. The poetry, epigrams, quotations, and excerpts are not merely anthologized illustrations—they are definitive. Our aim is to reassert the substantiveness of our literary legacy. It is to recover the meaning and the import of its blessing in our lives. Ours is a desire for a rediscovery of the profound joy of the shelf life—at both the level of visceral pleasure and to the extent of spiritual transformation.

Admittedly, this kind of book bears the inevitable stamp of subjective experience. That is by design. In fact, it belongs to a series of books published by Cumberland House, and it is designed to exposit some very personal passions. *Letters Home* deals with the sage counsel of bygone days; *Best Friends* explores the ways friendship shapes our lives; *Just Visiting* takes a look at the way travel has enlightened lives and viewpoints throughout history; *Lost Causes* discusses seemingly vanquished, yet always resolute convictions; *Christmas Spirit* recovers the true meaning of the Yuletide season; *Garden Graces* deals with the joys of the soil and its fruits; and *Sports Fan* delves into the peculiar pleasures afforded us by competition and games. Still to come are additional volumes on domesticity, music, handicrafts, architecture, food, and Eastertide.

By its very nature, this book—like all the others in the series—is more a testimony than a documentary. These are our passions, our traditions, and our sundry favorites. Our purpose in writing is to both express and profess. As the poet Tristan Gylberd once quipped, "Let my only protest be the fact that I may yet find joy in that which the world has rejected. Let my only manifesto be published in the depth of my happiness, the settledness of my home, and the satisfaction of my soul. Let my revelry in grace be my sternest rebuke to the restless nomad spirit of this age. Let my dance judge their dirge."

"A precious mouldering pleasure 'tis
To meet an antique book
In just the dress his century wore;
A privilege, I think,

"His venerable hand to take,
A warming in our own,
A passage back, or two, to make
To times when he was young.

"His quaint opinions to inspect,
His knowledge to unfold
On what concerns our mutual mind,
The literature of old.

"What impressed the scholars most,
What competitions ran
When Plato was a certainty
And Sophocles a man,

"When Sappho was a living girl,
And Beatrice wore
The gown that Dante deified.
Facts, centuries before.

"He traverses familiar,
As one should come to town
And tell you all your dreams were true:
He lived where dreams are sown.

"His presence is enchantment,
You beg him not to go;
His volumes shake their vellum heads
And tantalize just so."

Emily Dickinson (1830–1886)

Literary Affections

*R*eaders are quite happily a breed apart. It is not that they are elitists, snobs, or ivory tower parvenus. On the contrary, they are often the most down-to-earth enthusiasts in any given community at any given time. It is just that over the course of their lives they have developed a taste for quiet reflection and substantive expression. They have acquired the habits of inquisitiveness and thoughtfulness. They appreciate rip-roaring yarns as much as harmonious nuances of narration; they relish well-drawn characters as much as graceful and temperate prose; they celebrate redolent imagination as much as clear articulation. They love words, ideas, and stories. They love to laugh and cry. They yearn for grace and consolation. They care passionately about beauty, goodness, and truth. They are, indeed, a breed apart.

"A broad interest in books usually means a broad interest in life."

Lyman Abbott (1835–1922)

"The man who does not read good books has no advantage over the man who can't read them."

Mark Twain (1835–1910)

"This habit of reading, I make bold to tell you, is your pass to the greatest, the purest, and the most perfect pleasure that God has prepared for His creatures. It lasts when all other pleasures fade. It will support you when all other recreations are gone. It will last until your death. It will make your hours pleasant to you as long as you live."

Anthony Trollope (1815–1882)

"Books are the food of youth; the delight of old age; the ornament of prosperity; the refuge and comfort of adversity; a delight at home; no hindrance abroad; companions at night, in traveling, in the country. Indeed, no wise man ought ever be found apart their company."

&} *Cicero (106–43 B.C.)* {&

"I really believe you can't build a self without books. You get an inner voice by listening to someone else's words in your ear."

&} *Jane Hamilton (1957–)* {&

"The end of reading is not more books but more life."

&} *Holbrook Jackson (1874–1948)* {&

"It had been startling and disappointing to me to find out that storybooks had been written by people, that books were not natural wonders, coming up of themselves like grass. Yet regardless of where they came from, I cannot remember a time when I was not in love with them—with the books themselves, cover and binding and the paper they were printed on, with their smell and their weight and with their possession in my arms, captured and carried off to myself. Still illiterate, I was ready for them, committed to all the reading I could give them."

Eudora Welty (1909–)

"My early and invincible love of reading, I would not exchange for the treasures of India."

Edward Gibbon (1734–1794)

"No matter what his rank or position may be, the lover of books is the richest and the happiest of the children of men."

Alfred Johnson (1791–1877)

"There is no frigate like a book
To take us lands away
Nor any Coursers like a page
Of prancing poetry;
This traverse may be the poorest take
Without oppress of toll;
How frugal is the chariot
That bears the human soul."
                    ❧ *Emily Dickinson (1830–1886)* ☙

"You may perhaps be brought to acknowledge that it is very
well worthwhile to be tormented for two or three years of
one's life, for the sake of being able to read all the rest of it."
                    ❧ *Jane Austen (1775–1817)* ☙

"Of the making of books there is no end."
                    ❧ *King Solomon* ☙

"So rich is the companionship of books, so profound is the enrichment of books, and so deep is the pleasure of books that none of the vast changes in cultures and civilizations since has stemmed their ever rising tide."

Tristan Gylberd (1954–)

"Books are the wise man's passport to success and greatness. Books are the thresholds to wonder; the gateways to enlightenment; the foundations of virtue; and the pediment of honor."

Cicero (106–43 B.C.)

"Reading feeds the brain. It is evident that most minds are starving to death."

Benjamin Franklin (1706–1790)

"A well-read people are easy to lead, but difficult to drive; easy to govern, but difficult to enslave."

Baron Henry Brougham (1778–1868)

"Reading maketh a full man, conference a ready man, and writing an exact man."

Francis Bacon (1561–1626)

"Of all the diversions of life, there is none so proper to fill up its empty spaces as the reading of useful and entertaining authors."

Joseph Addison (1672–1719)

"What a joy there is in a good book, writ by some great master of thought, who breaks into beauty as in summer the meadow into grass and dandelions and violets with geraniums and manifold sweetness."
Herman Guenther (1799–1854)

"Every man who knows how to read has it in his power to magnify himself, to multiply the ways in which he exists, to make his life full, significant, and interesting."
Aldous Huxley (1894–1963)

"Reading is to the mind what exercise is to the body."
Richard Steele (1672–1729)

"Read at every wait; read at all hours; read within leisure; read about in times of labor; read as one goes in; read as one goes out. The task of the educated mind is simply put: read to lead."

Cicero (106–43 B.C.)

"Books have always a secret influence on the understanding; we cannot at pleasure obliterate ideas; he that reads books of science, though without any fixed desire of improvement, will grow more knowing; he that entertains himself with moral and religious treatises, will imperceptibly advance in goodness; the ideas which are often offered to the mind, will at last find a lucky moment when it is disposed to receive them."

Samuel Johnson (1709–1784)

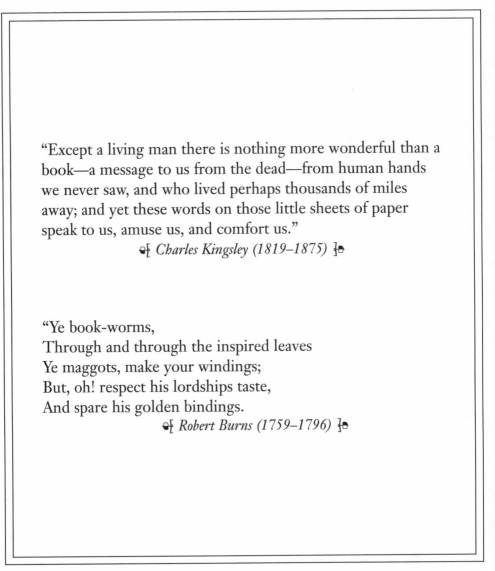

"Except a living man there is nothing more wonderful than a book—a message to us from the dead—from human hands we never saw, and who lived perhaps thousands of miles away; and yet these words on those little sheets of paper speak to us, amuse us, and comfort us."

Charles Kingsley (1819–1875)

"Ye book-worms,
Through and through the inspired leaves
Ye maggots, make your windings;
But, oh! respect his lordships taste,
And spare his golden bindings.

Robert Burns (1759–1796)

"Most ignorance is vincible ignorance; we don't know because we don't want to know; we remain uninformed because we refuse to read."

Aldous Huxley (1894–1963)

"Amusement is the satisfaction of those who cannot think; entertainment is the gratification of those who cannot read."

Alexander Pope (1688–1744)

Peculiarity and C. S. Lewis

"You can't get a cup of tea large enough or a book long enough to suit me."
C. S. LEWIS (1898–1963)

Long before the bane of television invaded our every waking moment, C. S. Lewis commented that, while most people in modern industrial cultures are at least marginally able to read, they just don't. In his wise and wonderful book *An Experiment in Criticism*, Lewis said, "The majority, though they are sometimes frequent readers, do not set much store by reading. They turn to it as a last resource. They abandon it with alacrity as soon as any alternative pastime turns up. It is kept for railway journeys, illnesses, odd moments of enforced solitude, or for the process called reading oneself to sleep. They sometimes combine it with desultory conversation; often, with listening to the radio. But literary people are always looking for leisure and silence in which to read and do so with their whole attention. When they are denied such attentive and undisturbed reading even for a few days they feel impoverished."

Lewis went further, admitting that there is a profound puzzlement on the part of the mass of the citizenry over the tastes and habits of the literate. "It is pretty clear that the majority," he wrote, "if they spoke without passion and were fully articulate, would not accuse us of liking the wrong books, but of making such a fuss about any books at all. We treat as a main ingredient in our well-being something which to them is marginal. Hence to say simply that they like one thing and we another is to leave out nearly the whole of the facts."

All this was not intended by Lewis to imply any hint of moral turpitude on the part of modern bohemianism; rather, it was simply to recognize the simple reality of the gaping chasm that exists between those who read and those who don't, between the popular many and the peculiar few. It was to recognize that the life he lived was a unique one—perhaps even a peculiar one, in these latter days.

The problem with serious reading, he realized, was part and parcel with virtually all the other problems of modernity—serious reading is often laborious work requiring unflinching discipline, and if there is anything that we moderns have an aversion to, it is disciplined work. In this odd to-whom-it-may-concern, instant-everything day of microwavable meals, prefab buildings, drive-through windows, no-wait credit approvals, and predigested formula-entertainment, we tend to want to reduce everything to the level of the least common denominator and the fastest turnaround—which seems to be getting lower and lower and faster and faster with every passing day.

Even the church has fallen prey to this spirit of the times. If we really had our druthers we wouldn't want worship to be too terribly demanding. We wouldn't want doctrine that challenges our pet notions. We really only want music that we're comfortable with. We only want preaching that reassures us, that reinforces our peculiar preferences, that affords us a sense of serenity—and all in record time. We want quick change; cheap grace; inspirational platitudes; bumper sticker theology; easy faith. We want Christianity Lite. We want the Nice News, not necessarily the Good News.

For the same reasons, when we read, most of us would really prefer literary junk food. The predigested factoids of *USA Today* are much easier to swallow than Cotton Mather's *Magnalia Christi Americana*. Face it, John Grisham, Danielle Steele, and Tom Clancy are easier to digest than William Shakespeare, John Milton, and G. K. Chesterton. Reading is a discipline—and all discipline is difficult. But then, that is the way it is with anything worthwhile, really.

In his remarkable book entitled *The Moral Sense*, James Q. Wilson drives home that point with great clarity. He argues that "the best things in life" invariably "cost us something." We must sacrifice to attain them, to achieve them, to keep them, even to enjoy them.

That is one of the most important lessons we can learn in life. It is the message that we know we ought to instill in our children: Patience, commitment, diligence, constancy, and discipline will ultimately pay off if we are willing to defer gratification long enough for the seeds we have sown to sprout and bear. A flippant, shallow, and imprecise approach to anything—be it sports or academics or the trades or business or marriage—is ultimately self-defeating. It is not likely to satisfy any appetite—at least, not for long.

Now, you might be thinking, "Gee, this is all rather obvious, isn't it? Serious reading as an essential element of cultural excellence and achievement? Of course."

All evidence, however, points to the fact that such a notion is anything but obvious. Just look at the agenda items on any proposal for educational reform—secular or Christian, day schooling or home schooling. You'll find recommendations on interactive media, computer software technology enhancements, comprehensive correlative curricula, outcome-based objectives, trade affinity matrices, life skills development, and turn-key textual exercises. But nothing—or next to nothing—about Chaucer, Mandeville, Coleridge, Cervantes, Melville, Hawthorne, Longfellow, Wordsworth, Dickens, Twain, or Warren.

The brilliant men and women who wove the fabric of western civilization knew nothing of correlative curricula or programmed outcomes or software enhancements—but they were well-read. And they were well-read in a way that we can only dream of today despite all our nifty gadgets, gimmicks, and bright ideas. They were steeped in Augustine, Dante, Plutarch, and Vasari. They were conversant in the ideas of Seneca, Ptolemy, Virgil, and Aristophanes. The notions of Athanasius, Chrysostom, Anselm, Bonaventure, Aquinas, Machiavelli, Abelard, and Wyclif informed their thinking and shaped their worldview. They thus were able to preserve and then to pass on to their progeny a heritage of real substance.

They read. They read widely. They read seriously. They read omnivorously.

C. S. Lewis was the happy heir of that great tradition. And he relished that fact. His brilliant writing—in his novels like *Till We Have Faces*, *The Lion, the Witch, and the Wardrobe*, *The Screwtape Letters*, and *Perelandra*, as well as in his nonfiction such as *The Four Loves*, *Surprised by Joy*, *The Abolition of Man*, and *A Grief Observed*—evidence voracious reading.

Lewis was born in 1898 and died in 1963, just seven days shy of his sixty-fifth birthday. He became renowned as a popular bestselling author, a brilliant English literary scholar and stylist, and one of the foremost apologists for the Christian faith. Recalling his formative childhood years, he wrote: "I am the product of long corridors, empty sunlit rooms, upstairs indoor silences, attics explored in solitude, distant noises of gurgling cisterns and pipes, and the noise of wind under the tiles. Also, of endless books. My father bought all the books he read and never got rid of any of them. There were books in the study, books in the drawing room, books in the cloakroom, books—two deep—in the great bookcase on the landing, books piled as high as my shoulder in the cistern attic, books of all kinds reflecting every transient stage of my parents' interest, books readable and unreadable, books suitable for a child and books most emphatically not. Nothing was forbidden me. In the seemingly endless rainy afternoons I took volume after volume from the shelves. I had always the same certainty of finding a book that was new to me as a man who walks into a field has of finding a new blade of grass."

Throughout his life, Lewis celebrated everything that is good and right and true about the literary life. The happy result was that he was larger than life in virtually every respect. Although he knew that this was little more than a peculiarity in the eyes of most, he did not chafe against it. Instead, he fully embraced it. He explained: "Those of us who have been true readers all our life seldom fully realize the enormous extension of our being which we owe to authors. We realize it best when we talk with an unliterary friend. He may be full of goodness and good sense but he inhabits a tiny world. In it, we should be suffocated. The man who is contented to be only himself, is in a prison. My own eyes are not enough for me. I will see through those of others." This is because, he argued, "Literary experience heals the wound, without undermining the privilege, of individuality. Here, as in worship, in love, in moral action, and in knowing, I transcend myself; and am never more myself than when I do."

Such peculiarity is glorious in every respect, precisely because it is so human.

A Practicum on Tea

"Now stir the fire, and close the shutters fast,
Let fall the curtains, wheel the sofa round,
And, while the bubbling and loud hissing urn
Throws up a steamy column, and the cups,
That cheer but not inebriate, wait on each,
So let us welcome, peaceful ev'ning in."
WILLIAM COWPER (1731-1800)

While Cowper's pastoral musings paint the picture of a storm-buffeted winter evening with family nestled safely inside strong walls, that particular tableau of domesticity is rarer and rarer today. Still, the readers' home will more often than others be the site of such tranquility. Why? Very simply, because reading won't compete with television. It will deign to coexist with music, it makes allowances for conversation and the urgent sharing of especially fine passages, but it will not allow the fraternity of the one-eyed monster, with its fascinating visual movement, its ever-altering volume, and lessened mental engagement. The television once ignited will always win out—it must be firmly extinguished or never set off at all if an evening of reading is ever to occur.

To make an evening's reading more inviting to all who pass through the room, sometimes crafty bait must be employed, and Cowper's cozy teatime vision can be consulted here. We like certain types of tea on cold winter evenings. Our children have always preferred hot chocolate. Occasionally we will have a flavored coffee. Shortbread or other nongreasy finger food—protect those pages—also contribute to the general softened atmosphere of a reading night. Here are some of our favorites:

- Several Celestial Seasonings or Republic of Tea blends are quite wonderful and readily available—chamomile, raspberry patch, cherry blackberry, and red zinger are our most frequent indulgences. Lots of other companies make great herbal teas, but what reader can resist those great Celestial Seasonings or Republic of Tea packages with all their epigrams, quotes, and trivia?

- Hot chocolate: Homemade is always best, and our most reliable source of never-fail recipes, *The Joy of Cooking*, lets us in on the secret:
  Combine, stir and boil for 2 minutes—in the top of a double boiler over direct but low heat:
  1 cup boiling water
  ¼ cup cocoa
  ⅛ t. salt
  2 to 4 T sugar

Then Add:

    ½ t. cinnamon (we never do)

    $\frac{1}{16}$ t. cloves and/or nutmeg (we omit this, as well)

Place the top of the boiler over boiling water.

Add: 3 cups scalded milk

Stir and heat the cocoa. Cover and keep over hot water for ten more minutes. Beat with a wire whisk before serving.

- Now to be perfectly frank, more often than not we use instant hot-chocolate mixes in our home these days, but homemade cocoa more often found a place in those glowing evenings of our children's childhoods.

- As with most things culinary, presentation matters. We have ugly plastic cups in our kitchen just like most moderns, but when an evening of reading is really possible in our busy schedules, we drink our tea from sturdy handcrafted ceramic mugs. Why not from fine china cups? Simply put, they require too frequent refilling. Who wants to leave an interesting moment every fifteen minutes to refill a delicate cup? Leave those for daytime snatches of reading, but bring out the large, reliable mug for evenings.

- Cowper speaks of inebriation. Actually, inebriation should never occur at all, but even a little dulling of the senses does no one any good when all faculties should be alert and engaged in the book at hand.

Literary Habits

*L*iterary affections naturally give way to literary habits. People who love to read will find the time to read—the distractions of life are simply crowded out. Even amidst the tyranny of the urgent, which seems the natural accompaniment to modern life, readers seem to be able to catch moments of quiet, snatches of solitude, brief interludes of attentiveness to the ideas and ideals of literature. Invariably, this relentless prioritizing of time leads to a necessary prioritizing of content.

At some point every serious reader comes to the realization that he will never be able to read everything he wishes to, and so turns his attention to read everything he ought to—he refocuses his attentions on the enduring masterworks: the classics.

"A life being very short, and the quiet hours of it few, we ought to waste none of them in reading valueless books."

John Ruskin (1819–1900)

"The simplest explanation for the survival of the classics is that ordinary readers have found them worth preserving."

Moses Hadas (1890–1966)

"A classic is a book that has never finished saying what it has to say."

Italo Calvino (1923–1985)

"When you reread a classic you do not see more in the book than you did before; you see more in you than was there before. A classic is a mirror that reflects the truest self—and all the more clearly than the mere looking glasses of our own vain manufacture."

Charles Gillespie (1888–1962)

"A book is a mirror: if an ass peers into it, you can't expect an apostle to look out."

George Christoph Lichtenberg (1742–1799)

"I don't think you can read a hundred pages of any of the true classics before you start feeling that unmistakable shiver up and down your spine that tells you you're reading a timeless work."

Thomas Chalmers (1780–1847)

"One must not think that feeling is everything. Art is nothing without form. The classics teach us that vital lesson."
Gustave Flaubert (1821–1880)

"Most editors are failed writers—but so are most writers. That is why it is always best, when in doubt, to read the classics. There time has done all the sorting for you."
T. S. Eliot (1888–1965)

"In the case of good books, the point is not to see how many of them you can get through, but rather how many can get through to you."
Mortimer Adler (1902–)

"No book that will not improve by repeated readings deserves to be read at all."
Thomas Carlyle (1795–1881)

"A classic, according to the usual definition, is an old author canonized by admiration, and an authority in his particular style. At first the only true classics for moderns were the ancients. But a true classic today, as I should like to hear it defined, is an author who has enriched the human mind, increased its treasure, and caused it to advance a step; who has discovered some moral and not equivocal truth, or revealed some eternal passion in that heart where all seemed known and discovered; who has expressed his thought, observation, or invention, in no matter what form, only provided it be broad and great, refined and sensible, sane and beautiful in itself; who has spoken to all in his own peculiar style, a style which is found to be also that of the whole world, a style new without neologism, new and old, easily contemporary with all time. Such a classic may for a moment have been revolutionary; it may at least have seemed so, but it is not; it only lashed and subverted whatever prevented the restoration of the balance of order and beauty."

Charles Augustin Sainte-Beuve (1804–1869)

"A classic evinces purity of taste, propriety of terms, variety of expression, attentive care in suiting the diction to the thought, and over all a distinctive character all its own."
Marquis de Remusat (1791–1855)

"I call the classical healthy, and the romantic sickly. In my opinion the Nibelungen song is as much a classic as Homer. Both are healthy and vigorous. The works of the day are romantic, not because they are new, but because they are weak, ailing, or sickly. Ancient works are classical not because they are old, but because they are powerful, fresh, and healthy. If we regarded the romantic and classical from those two points of view, we should soon all agree."
Johann Goethe (1749–1834)

"Ever since civilized man has had a literature he has appar-
ently sought to make selections from it and thus put his
favorite passages together in a canon—these then are the
classics."

Henry Cabot Lodge (1850–1924)

"In the Golden Age a book
Was then, in fact, a Book
Where a wistful man might look
And finding something through the whole
Was a beating—like a human soul."

Richard le Gallienne (1866–1901)

"There is a great deal of difference between the eager man who wants to read a book and the tired man who wants a book to read. A man reading a Le Quex mystery wants to get to the end of it. A man reading the Dickens novel wished that it might never end."

George MacDonald (1824–1905)

"Mediocre minds usually dismiss anything which reaches beyond their own understanding."

Duc de la Rochefoucauld (1613–1680)

"You can find all the new ideas in the old books; only there you will find them balanced, kept in their place, and sometimes contradicted and overcome by other and better ideas. The great writers did not neglect a fad because they had not thought of it, but because they had thought of it and of all the answers to it as well."

G. K. Chesterton (1874–1936)

"I hate to read new books. There are twenty or thirty volumes that I have read over and over again, and these are the only ones that I have any desire ever to read at all. Some judge books as they do fashions or complexions, which are admired only in their newest gloss. That is not my way. I do not think altogether the worse of a book for having survived the author a generation or two. I have more confidence in the dead than the living. Contemporary writers may generally be divided into two classes—one's friends or one's foes. Of the first we are compelled to think too well, and of the last we are disposed to think too ill, to receive much genuine pleasure from the perusal, or to judge fairly of the merits of either."

William Hazlitt (1778–1830)

"The oldest books are still only just out to those who have not yet read them."

Samuel Butler (1835–1902)

CLASSICS AND J. M. DENT

"When I was about ten or eleven years old I formed the habit of reading which has never since been broken. I developed peculiar literary affections and habits which inevitably generated an insatiable appetite for the classic masterworks then passing into popular disfavor. My career was thus established not upon any market sensibility, but upon my own predilection to preserve the good, the true, and the beautiful."
JOSEPH MALABY DENT (1849–1926)

Mark Twain once defined a literary classic as "a book which people praise but don't read." Fortunately, Joseph Malaby Dent, founder of J. M. Dent & Sons, never took that quip to heart. Over the course of his career he probably did more than any other single individual to inculcate a popular appreciation for the classics—his Everyman's Library editions, provided excellent translations in durable bindings at extraordinarily cheap prices. Walk into almost any used bookshop in the English-speaking world today and there is apt to be a whole section filled with the little volumes that throughout the first half of the twentieth century became synonymous with the literary life.

Born in the old English village of Darlington, he was the tenth child of George Dent, a housepainter. As a youngster, he received elementary instruction at a local grammar school that emphasized little more than basic reading and writing skills. But by the time he was thirteen, he had already entered the workforce as a printer's apprentice. Shortly thereafter, he turned to bookbinding. A voracious reader, he became especially enamored with the classics—the ragged old volumes he was most likely called upon to rebind.

In 1867 Dent moved to London, where he set up his own bookbinding shop. He quickly gained a reputation for fine craftsmanship; indeed, his customers frequently rued the fact that his fine leather bindings put to shame the unattractive Victorian typography of the sheets they bound.

Encouraged by his rather elite clientel, Dent founded his publishing business in 1888. His first production, *Charles Lamb's Essays of Elia*, was edited by Augustine Birrell and illustrated by Herbert Railton. In 1889 he published an edition of *Goldsmith's Poems and Plays*. Works by Jane Austen, the Brontë sisters, Geoffrey Chaucer, Daniel Defoe, Maria Edgeworth, Henry Fielding, Samuel Johnson, Lord Tennyson, and W. B. Yeats followed between 1889 and 1894. All of these early editions were expensively produced in limited quantities on handmade paper.

Nevertheless, they enjoyed remarkable following among the literary cognoscenti.

In 1893 the bookseller Frederick Evans suggested that Dent publish a series of pocket volumes of William Shakespeare's plays. Although there did not seem to be much demand for cheap editions of the classics—in fact, sales of the great books had suffered a serious and steady decline throughout the latter half of the Victorian Age—Dent decided to follow the inclinations of his own heart and mind. He established the Temple Shakespeare series in 1894. The series was an almost immediate success—eventually it included forty volumes that were sold for a mere one shilling a volume. Over the next four decades the series sold more than five million copies, the largest sale made in Shakespeare since the plays were written.

Shortly thereafter, Dent began publishing other titles under the Mediaeval Towns series, the Temple Dramatists series, the Lyric Poets series, and the Temple Biographies—all were inexpensive reprints of long-neglected classic works. By 1895 Dent had published about three hundred volumes and paid off all his debts.

In 1904, with years of experience publishing classics at popular prices, Dent began to flesh out his ambitious vision for the Everyman's Library. It was to be a series of one thousand classics—practically the whole canon of western civilization's great books—sold at an affordable price. Production began in 1906, and more than a hundred fifty titles were issued by the end of that first year.

Although the experts had decreed that the classics were dry, uninspiring, and hardly suited for the fast-paced industrial world of the twentieth century, Dent demonstrated that properly presented, the great books were as appealing as ever. He believed this was due to the fact that while the classics exhibit distinguished style, fine artistry, and keen intellect, they also create a whole universe of imagination and thought. Secondly, unlike the simplistic nursery tales manifest in the literature of modernity, he believed the classics portrayed life as complex and multifaceted, depicting both negative and positive aspects of human character in the process of discovering and testing enduring virtues. Third, he believed that the classics had an inevitable transforming effect on the reader's self-understanding—stretching, shaping, and confronting him. Fourth, he thought they invited and rewarded frequent rereadings—they were always new. Fifth, they had the uncanny ability to adapt themselves to various times and places, and thus they provided a sense of the shared life of humanity over the course of space and time. Finally, he held that their mere endurance across all the varied times and seasons of human experience demonstrated an interminable permanence amid modern temporality that was simultaneously comforting and challenging.

Although the venture was obviously a commercial risk, Dent was confident that the very thing that made the classics classic would ensure success for the series. He was right. Public demand for books in Everyman's Library exceeded every expectation.

Within a few years of its triumphant launch, however, the momentum of Everyman's Library was interrupted by World War I. The seven hundredth volume of the Everyman's Library had been reached in 1914, but within a few months after the outbreak of hostilities, the publication of additional volumes was halted. Wartime inflation and shortages of supplies more than doubled the price of each volume. After the war, inflation and shortages actually worsened. By 1921 new titles again began to appear but only in a slow trickle.

Dent responded to the setbacks by expanding book sales to international markets. He established a French subsidiary, which distributed Everyman books in France, translated the classics into French, and published various French titles in the Collection Gallia series. He expanded international distribution to North America by setting up a Canadian subsidiary and by allowing E. P. Dutton to distribute Everyman titles throughout the United States. In addition, Dent hired agents to sell Everyman titles in Australia, New Zealand, South Africa, and most of continental Europe.

The Everyman's Library finally reached the millennial volume with the publication of Aristotle's *Metaphysics* in 1956. In just fifty years total sales of the Everyman's series had exceeded sixty million copies of the classics.

Though his company was finally sold by his heirs in 1988, almost exactly a century after he founded it, the impact of the little publisher that dared stand against the tide of the modern conventions of uniformity, conformity, and efficiency is still felt. Joseph Dent's literary habits reintroduced the pertinence, puissance, and propriety of the classics to a world all too desperate for permanent things.

A Practicum on Reading Aloud

" 'Dear Pig, are you willing to sell for one shilling
Your ring?' Said the Piggy, 'I will.'
So they took it away, and were married next day
By the Turkey who lives on the hill.
They dined on mince, and slices of quince,
Which they ate with a runcible spoon;
And hand in hand, on the edge of the sand,
They danced by the light of the moon,
The moon,
The moon,
They danced by the light of the moon."
EDWARD LEAR (1812–1888)

Silent reading is a fairly modern innovation. As late as the eighteenth century, it was thought that the best way to truly appreciate the classics was to read them aloud—all the better to relish
the beauty of the words, the music of the composition, and the
architecture of the ideas. Of course, the classics are not limited
to great philosophical tomes by the likes of Aristotle, Augustine,
and Aquinas. In fact, some of the greatest classic works ever

written are books for children—books that are at their best when read aloud.

The best thing about reading aloud to children, aside from developmental progress and all that good stuff, is onomatopoeia. "Clang, clang!" "Harrumph!" "Chugga-chugga" "Choo-Choo" "Splat" "Ring! Ring!" "Flutter, Flutter." Wonderful children's literature doesn't just progress along the pages in staid font transferring information, it sings out from the very book at us! Be it Mike Mulligan's steam shovel digging away furiously or Peter Rabbit hopping lippity, lippity through Mr. MacGregor's dangerous garden patch, we are fully engaged from once-upon-a-time to everyone-lived-happily-ever-after. Ducks wear poke bonnets, trains wish desperately to make children happy, dreams come true, elephants and carpets fly, and small children affect the outcome of their worlds. Adults who wear business attire and behave perfectly appropriately in steel and glass towers day after monotonous day transform themselves into snakes, mean old hags, princesses with snooty accents, and sorrowful baby bears when a small child is snuggled on their lap with a good book. Is it any wonder that a happy child's evening litany includes "Read one more book, please?"

Children's classics are those books that can be read over and over and over again, with great anticipation and satisfaction. Character traits that would serve well both presidents and street sweepers are inculcated between the few pages, and good, while often tattered, does overcome evil in the end. Lost battles are still worth the fight. As in real life, the honor and import of the struggle count more than winning.

- Do you miss it? If so, rush out to a neighborhood school and ask for the privilege to read to some children once a week. Better yet, ask for the greater privilege of being a volunteer tutor in a local school and teaching someone to read. The rewards of macaroni necklaces, somewhat sticky hugs, detailed stories of the day's adventures, and glittery homemade cards can be as touching as the gifts bestowed on you by your loved ones. There's also the quiet inner assurance that you are making a permanent difference in the world.

- Rather than purchasing huge quantities of books for your children, purchase quality copies of some great ones, and read these over and over again.

- Reading quietly to a small child in the tub just before the dinner hour has a calming effect on the entire household.

- Do you have one of those busy little people in your family who finds it very difficult to sit still? They really can concentrate better on the story you're reading if they have a crayon and paper in front of them or a small car to hold in their hands as you read.

- Keep wonderful books such as *The Chronicles of Narnia* in the car and read aloud to the entire family if you have a regular long commute together or if you will be together on vacation.
- Make sure each child has a bookshelf or space on the family bookshelf of his or her own. Books should never be kept in toyboxes, where they will be destroyed. Treat them as the treasures they are.
- Your children must see you reading if they are to take reading seriously themselves.
- Perhaps you missed out on many wonderful children's classics as a child. Buy them and read them, then donate the books to area school libraries or create a small library at a shelter for kids in transitional housing. Any schoolteacher can provide you with the name of a young student who needs and would appreciate a book for Christmas.
- If you have more than one child in your family, their reading skills will vary. Some children simply don't read well; it is work for them, and not unadulterated joy. For these children especially, reading aloud to them for as many years as they will listen is especially important for their cultural understanding and development. Things as simple as the inflection in your voice when you read about an inappropriate action by a

character will imprint upon your child's moral character, if he or she is read to often.

- Some children simply aren't as affectionate as others. They often get left out when it comes to reading time merely because it isn't as sensuously enjoyable for everyone as with a snuggling sweetheart engaged in the story. These children need your patience and time even more than others, who will probably find ways to get their needs met in life through normal daily interaction. Do whatever it takes to keep their attention: feed them cookies, let them blow bubbles, and concentrate on rhyming, fast-moving stories and beautiful illustrations. You might be the only person in their entire life who will take the time to interest them in books. A lot of extra stimulation is not advised, however, for a child easily read to. Imagination develops in wonderful ways when pure listening skills are employed.

Literary Places

*M*ost readers can read almost anywhere—we've read on planes and trains, in courtrooms and classrooms, in laundromats and grocery lines, on sandy beaches and in busy airports. But given our druthers, most of us would probably prefer a nice little corner by the hearthside with a steaming mug of java in hand, or perhaps in an overstuffed library chair with an ottoman and a stack of books at our side, or maybe even out on a screened-in porch with a ceiling fan stirring the summer stillness and a dripping glass of lemonade at the ready. There is just something about a space set aside just for reading to entice us to plunge into a rich text, to focus all our attentions on a complex passage, or to ponder anew the wonder of evocative verse.

"I have sought for happiness everywhere, but I have found it nowhere except in a little corner with a little book."
Thomas á Kempis (1379–1471)

"Perhaps the greatest gift any father can bestow upon his children, apart from the covenant blessings of parish life and a comprehension of the doctrines of grace, is a passion for reading. It is cheap, it consoles, it distracts, it excites, it gives a knowledge of the world, and it offers experience of a wide kind. Indeed, it is nothing less than a moral illumination."
Thomas Chalmers (1780–1847)

"A little library, growing every year, is an honorable part of a man's history. It is a man's duty to have books. A library is not a luxury, but one of the necessaries of life. Be certain that your house is adequately and properly furnished—with books rather than with furniture. Both if you can, but books at any rate."
Henry Ward Beecher (1813–1887)

"Sitting last winter among my books, and walled round with all the comfort and protection which they and my fireside could afford me—to wit, a table of high-piled books at my back, my writing desk to one side of me, some shelves on the other, and the feeling of the warm fire at my feet—I began to consider how I loved the authors of those books; how I loved them too, not only for the imaginative pleasures they have afforded me, but for their making me love the very books themselves, and delight to be in contact with them. I looked sideways at my Spencer, my Theocritus, and my Arabian Nights; then above at my Italian poets; then behind me at my Dryden and Pope, my romances, and my Boccaccio; then on my left side at my Chaucer, who lay on my writing desk; and thought how natural it was in Charles Lamb to give a kiss to an old folio, as I once saw him do to Chapman's Homer."

Leigh Hunt (1784–1859)

"The familiar faces of my books welcomed me. I threw myself into my reading chair and gazed around me with pleasure. All my old friends present—there in spirit, ready to talk with me any moment when I was in the mood, making no claim upon my attention when I was not."

George MacDonald (1824–1905)

"Find the most comfortable position: seated, stretched out, curled up, or lying flat. Stretch your legs, go ahead and put your feet on a cushion, on two cushions, on the arms of the sofa, on the wings of the chair, on the coffee table, on the desk, on the piano, on the globe. Take your shoes off first. Adjust the light so you don't strain your eyes. Do it now, because once you're absorbed in reading there will be no budging you."

Italo Calvino (1923–1985)

"Just the knowledge that a good book is waiting at the end of a long day invariably makes that day happier."

Martha Gullik (1899–1972)

"Only one hour in the normal day is more pleasurable than the hour spent in bed with a book before going to sleep, and that is the hour spent in bed with a book after being called in the morning."

⋛ *Rose Macauley (1881–1958)* ⋚

"A small breakfast-room adjoined the drawing room, I slipped in there. It contained a bookcase: I soon possessed myself of a volume, taking care that it should be one stocked with pictures. I mounted into the window-seat: gathering up my feet, I sat cross-legged, like a Turk; and, having drawn the red moreen curtain nearly closed, I was shrined in double retirement. Folds of scarlet drapery shut in my view to the right hand; to the left were the clear panes of glass, protecting, but not separating me from the drear November day. At intervals while turning the leaves of my book, I studied the aspect of that winter afternoon. Afar, it offered a pale blank of mist and cloud; near a scene of wet lawn and storm-beat shrub, with ceaseless rain sweeping away wildly before a long and lamentable blast."

⋛ *Charlotte Brontë (1816–1855)* ⋚

"My father had left a small collection of books in a little room upstairs, to which I had access (for it adjoined my own) and which nobody else in our house ever troubled. From that blessed little room, Roderick Random, Peregrine Pickle, Humphrey Clinker, Tom Jones, the Vicar of Wakefield, Don Quixote, Gil Blas, and Robinson Crusoe came out, a glorious host, to keep me company. They kept alive my fancy, and my hope of something beyond that place and time—they, and the Arabian Nights and the Tales of the Genii—and did me no harm; for whatever harm was in some of them was not there fore me; I knew nothing of it. It is astonishing to me now, how I found time, in the midst of my porings and blunderings over heavier themes, to read those books as I did. This was my only and my constant comfort. When I think of it, the picture always rises in my mind, of a summer evening, the boys at play in the churchyard, and I sitting on my bed reading as if for life."

Charles Dickens (1812–1870)

"I am the product of long corridors, empty sunlit rooms, upstairs indoor silences, attics explored in solitude, distant noises of gurgling cisterns and pipes, and the noise of wind under the tiles. Also, of endless books. My father bought all the books he read and never got rid of any of them. There were books in the study, books in the drawing room, books, in the cloakroom, books—two deep—in the great bookcase on the landing, books piled as high as my shoulder in the cistern attic, books of all kinds reflecting every transient stage of my parents' interest, books readable and unreadable, books suitable for a child and books most emphatically not. Nothing was forbidden me. In the seemingly endless rainy afternoons I took volume after volume from the shelves. I had always the same certainty of finding a book that was new to me as a man who walks into a field has of finding a new blade of grass."
C. S. Lewis (1898–1963)

"A home without books is like a room without windows."
Henry Ward Beecher (1813–1887)

"There are peculiar joys attached to the implements of reading. When we collect books, we are collecting happiness. When we build up a little library, we are bolstering the delight of life."

Zeno Philaton (1697–1742)

"For lovers of books, a house without books is no house at all; and in a family where books make a great part of the pleasure of living, they must be where they can be got at without trouble, and what is of more importance, where they can share in the life about them and receive some touches of humanity they supply and feed."

Clarence Cook (1822–1886)

"My books! I cannot tell you what they are to me—silent, wealthy, loyal, lovers. I do thank God for my books with every fiber of my being. I see them all just at my elbow now—Plato, Wordsworth, Myers, Bradley, Halburton, St. Augustine, Browning, Tennyson, Amiel, and the others."

Oswald Chambers (1874–1917)

"There are three services which books may render in the home: they may be ornaments, tools, or friends. In the best homes they are all three simultaneously."

Lyman Abbot (1835–1922)

QUIETNESS AND WINSTON CHURCHILL

"If you cannot read all your books, at any rate handle, or as it were, fondle them—peer into them, let them fall open where they will, read from the first sentence that arrests the eye, set them back on the shelves with your own hands, arrange them on your own plan so that you at least know where they are. Let them be your friends; let them be your acquaintances."
WINSTON CHURCHILL (1874–1965)

Chartwell was his refuge and sanctuary. The odd conglomeration of structures and additions on the Kentish weald, southeast of London was, for him, an earthly paradise. In fact, he often asserted that "A day away from Chartwell is a day wasted." It was home.

And if ever a man needed a home, an earthly elysium to recharge, recoup, and reinvigorate, it was Winston Churchill.

He was born into privilege in 1874 as the son of the parliamentary master, Lord Randolph Churchill, and thus one of the heirs of the Marlborough legacy. Educated at Harrow and Sandhurst, he entered the Imperial service as a hussars officer. After notable tours of duty in India, Sudan, and South Africa, he entered parliament himself.

Having already made a name for himself, Churchill rose quickly through the political ranks. By 1908 he moved from the back benches to become president of the board of trade. Two years later he became home secretary. The next year he was appointed first lord of the admiralty presiding over the naval expansion that preceded the First World War. He was evidently a man of extraordinary gifts and abilities.

A series of disastrous defeats—including the failure of the Dardanelles expedition, which he had championed—Churchill lost his admiralty post and served out the remainder of the war on the front lines in France.

He undertook a painstakingly slow and difficult political rehabilitation in the years that followed, eventually serving as colonial secretary and chancellor of the exchequer. His parliamentary speeches were models of political prose. His writing was not only prolific, it was profound. His influence became enormous. But he once again fell into disfavor when the British Empire was caught in the throes of the Great Depression.

For a decade he was out of office. Most analysts believed his career was essentially over—he was now relegated to the outer fringe of political influence. His dire warnings of the threat from Hitler's Nazi regime in Germany went entirely unheeded.

During those difficult years, Churchill bought and renovated the old estate of Chartwell. It was a place where he could rest and reflect, read and write, paint and build, garden and walk. He once asserted that "We shape our dwellings and afterwards, our dwellings shape us." There can be little doubt that he shaped Chartwell to suit his peculiar interests and concerns.

Besides an expansive library, a mammoth study, a painting studio, and several isolated garden follies where he could go to be alone to think, Churchill dug ponds and pools, installed benches throughout the gardens, and staked out various spots around and throughout the house for reading—different places for different types of reading. Always an avid reader, he felt that different kinds of reading necessitated different kinds of environments.

For instance, he often read contemporary journalism and political dispatches in his study, which was suitably designed for such serious work. But he read history and biographies in the library, where the atmosphere was much more appropriately anti-quarian. He read hymns, ballads, and verse in the bright morning room downstairs—in the domain of his beloved wife, Clementine. He generally read great oratory aloud by the fish pond. And he read thrillers and mysteries in his studio.

There were great open hearths to read by in the winter and little window niches to read by in the spring. There were great leather club chairs to curl up in beside the library stacks and soft overstuffed divans in the living areas on which to stretch out. Everywhere, there were bright lamps so that every corner invited reading, reflection, conversation, and contemplation.

Churchill's intention was to create comfortable and distinctive spaces in his home and throughout the property that invoked the spirit of the activity that would take place there. He was naturally a collector—he had book collections, art collections, hat collections, medal collections, autograph collections, stamp collections, uniform collections, scientific instrument collections, gun collections, and memento collections. So he filled the house and grounds with the distinctive—and often eccentric—marks of his passions. All these things, and the memorabilia that inevitably accompanied them, made the house uniquely his. There has hardly ever been a home that more immediately speaks of the man who owned it than Chartwell.

When the Second World War broke out, the hapless prime minister, Neville Chamberlain, was forced to bring Churchill into the government—even though he was now sixty-five years old. He was appointed first lord of the admiralty. The following May, when Chamberlain was forced to resign, Churchill was asked by the king to form a new government and accept the office of prime minister.

Over the next five years, he stood practically alone against the Nazi menace. Almost single-handedly he saved western civilization, stirring the British people to unimaginable feats of valor with his bold oratory and even bolder leadership. His unflagging energy and his stubborn refusal to make peace until Adolf Hitler was crushed were crucial in turning the tide of the war and ultimately leading the Western Allies to victory.

After the war, he returned to Chartwell. But he did not rest on his laurels. Long after most men sought retirement, Churchill continued to issue forth with prophetic books, speeches, and policy pronouncements—warning against the new threat of Communism's Iron Curtain, the isolation and fragmentation of ideological nationalism, and the unimaginable horrors of nuclear proliferation. Until Churchill's death in 1965, his home was a sanctuary amid the frenetic activity of his public life.

Extraordinary vitality, imagination, and boldness characterized his whole career. But, he was the first to admit, if he had not had Chartwell—its libraries and gardens, its nooks and crannies, its hearthsides and hedgerows, its peace and quiet—he would never have been able to be what he was called to be or do what he was called to do.

A Practicum on Homemaking

*"It seems to me that, whether it is recognized or not, there is a terrific
frustration which increases in intensity and harmfulness as time goes
on, when people are always daydreaming of the kind of place in which
they would like to live, yet never making the place where they do live
into anything artistically satisfying to them. Always to dream of a cot-
tage by a brook, while never doing anything original to the stuffy
boarding-house room in a city; always to dream of a rock, glass, and
timber house on the cliffs above the sea, while never putting anything of
yourself into the small village brick house; or to dream of what you
could do with a hut in the jungle yet never to think of your inherited
family mansion as anything but a place to mark time, is to waste creativity in this very basic area, and to hinder future creativity by not
allowing it to grow and develop through use. Trying out all the ideas
that come to you, within the limits of your present place, money, talents,
materials and so forth, will not use up everything you want to save for
the future, but will rather generate and develop more ideas."*

EDITH SCHAEFFER (1914–)

Edith Schaeffer's book *Hidden Art* redefined our newly married
philosophy of homemaking. In the time it took to read one short
book, our definition of homemaking changed from "cleaning

house" (hausfrau) to that of creating an environment which beckoned others, was comfortable, stimulating as a learning environment, and reflected the personalities of those dwelling in our home—instead of a trend or a decorator's impression of who we are. We like books, and we have them everywhere one could possibly park oneself to read—in the bedrooms, the hallway, the dining room, and the den. And our offices. Oh my, they're in the laundry room, too.

Creating a home environment that is both conducive to reading and is magnetically inviting to a book lover is really relatively simple. The adventures may be found within the two covers of the book; but the soft chair, the right lighting, and a table nearby for a beverage and maybe reading glasses must be "just so." While we may have books available all over the home, we've made room in every home we've lived in for a couple of reading spots. These are the elements found in every little reading center we've ever created in our homes along the way:

- Comfortable, but not reclining, seating—after all, we're creating a reading spot, not a literary napping facility. Find chairs that are comfortable for short and long legs, and use ottomans or stools.
- Floor lamps or lamps on higher furniture which distribute light from a little above and to one side of the reader are essential.

- A side table for beverages, reading glasses, and the stack of reading material is always appreciated by serious readers—that way everything is right at hand. It is even better if the table has a drawer for a highlighter or quote notebook.
- Consider the character of the readers. Are they drawn to a frilly floral print on the chair, or a leather, barn-siding, and aromatic pipe environment? Our own formula is 1) save up and find a great chair at an antique store or flea market; 2) save up and buy great upholstery for that particular chair; 3) save up and have the chair reupholstered just to your taste, and 4) shoo the dog off the newly upholstered, extremely comfortable chair!
- The kitchen is the heart of the home. Is there room for a window seat or a cozy nook hospitable for reading while something is bubbling on the stovetop? Would a child be comfortable reading aloud to Mom while dinner is cooking? How about one deep wicker chair with a soft cushion to inspire a little cookbook perusing?
- We have seating where we can read, write, and reflect all around the back yard, the front yard, and on the front porch. Our absolutely favorite place and time to read is early in the morning from April through June and then again from September until the cold weather sets in, on our own front porch. After our usual morning walk, we sit with a cup of hazelnut coffee, Bible

in lap, disturbed only by the motion at one of our birdfeeders or birdhouses, cats rubbing our ankles, or dogs jealously vying for attention. Our own little Eden, we prepare our hearts for the day—and our children can usually tell the difference!

Literary Collections

*L*ibraries are among the chief evidences of a civilized society. They are, in a very real sense great catalogs of human cultural achievement, paeans to art, music, literature, and ideas where all that really matters in life may be expressed and disseminated in accord with beauty, goodness, and truth. They are great piazzas where the conversations of the ages continue unabated. Best of all, they are accessible to anyone and everyone—the riches of libraries are available to all those who would but venture in to partake of their knowledge, understanding, and wisdom. For any reader, a visit to a really well-stocked library must necessarily be something akin to Coleridge's imagined visit to Kubla Khan's famed pleasure dome.

"We had that peculiar thrill which comes from going into a room redolent with the faint mustiness of old calf and feeling that almost any volume may turn out to be a treasure."
◦{ Harold Laski (1893–1950) }◦

"The studious silence of the library is but tranquil brightness."
◦{ James Joyce (1882–1941) }◦

"Educated men are as much superior to uneducated men as the living are to the dead. Collections of wisdom ought to be our aim, if our hope is to truly live."
◦{ Aristotle (384–322 B.C.) }◦

"The investigation of the meaning of words and their collective composition in literature is the beginning of true knowledge."

Antisthenes (c. 445–365 B.C.)

"Books are a delightful society. If you go into a room filled with books, even without taking them down from their shelves, they seem to speak to you, to welcome you."

William Gladstone (1809–1898)

"Come, and take a choice of all my library;
And so beguile thy sorrow."

William Shakespeare (c. 1564–1616)

"There is a time when nations emerging from barbarity and falling into regular subordination gain leisure to grow wise and feel the shame of ignorance and the craving pain of unsatisfied curiosity. To this hunger of the mind plain sense is grateful; that which fills the void removes uneasiness, and to be free from pain for a while is pleasure; but repletion generates fastidiousness, a saturated intellect soon becomes luxurious, and knowledge finds no willing reception till it is recommended by artificial diction. Thus it will be found as learning advances that in all nations the first writers are simple and that every age improves in elegance. One refinement makes way for another, and what was expedient to Virgil was necessary to Pope."

◦｛ *Samuel Johnson (1709–1784)* ｝◦

"Designing a library is one of the grandest things a man can do. But settling in to read in one is grander still. They are the epitome of civilization for they are the culmination of all that is good and right and true in a civilization."

ᛏ *Michael Graves (1939–)* ᛒ

"Any ordinary man can surround himself with two thousand books and thenceforward have at least one place in the world in which it is possible to be entirely happy."

ᛏ *Augustine Birrell (1850–1933)* ᛒ

"I have always imagined that Paradise will be a kind of library."

ᛏ *Jorge Luis Borges (1899–1986)* ᛒ

"Who kills a man kills a reasonable creature, God's image; but he who destroys a good book, kills reason itself, kills the image of God, as it were in the eye. Many a man lives a burden to the earth; but a good book is the precious life-blood of a master spirit, embalmed and treasured up on purpose to a life beyond life."

John Milton (1608–1674)

"My education was the liberty I had to read indiscriminately and all the time, with my eyes hanging out."

Dylan Thomas (1914–1953)

"If fortune turns her face once more in kindness upon me before I go, I may chance, some quiet day, to lay my over-beating temples on a book, and so have the death I most envy."

Leigh Hunt (1784–1859)

"O, let my books be then the eloquence
And dumb presagers of my speaking breast;
Who plead for live and for recompense
More than that tongue that hath more express'd"
⋅{ *William Shakespeare (c. 1564–1616)* }⋅

"It is from books that wise men derive consolation in the troubles of life."
⋅{ *Victor Hugo (1802–1885)* }⋅

"Modern art is what happens when painters stop looking at girls and persuade themselves that they have a better idea. The modern novel is that absurd mistake taken even further into the realm of madness."
⋅{ *John Ciardi (1916–1986)* }⋅

"But words are things, and a small drop of ink, falling like dew, upon a thought, produces that which makes thousands, perhaps millions, think."
Lord Byron (1788–1824)

"A library is a token of, nay, a trophy of grace."
Martin Luther (1483–1546)

"No place affords a more striking conviction of the vanity of human hopes than a public library."
Samuel Johnson (1709–1784)

"Today's mass culture would not know an idea, subversive or otherwise, if it met one. It traffics instead in sensibility and image, with a premium on the degrading: rap lyrics in which women are for using and abusing, movies in which violence is administered with a smirk and a smile. Casual cruelty, knowing sex. Nothing could be better designed to rob youth of its most ephemeral gift: innocence. The ultimate effect of our mass culture is to make children older than their years, to turn them into the knowing, cynical pseudo-adult that is by now the model kid of the TV sitcom. It is a crime against children to make them older than their years. And it won't do for the purveyors of cynicism to hide behind the First Amendment. Of course they have the right to publish and peddle this trash to kids. But they should have the decency not to. Let us therefore take a pledge, a stand, a covenant, against such rubbish, and recommit ourselves to the great civilizing impulse that gave rise to such things as libraries."

Charles Krauthammer (1939–)

"The very existence of libraries affords the best evidence that we may yet have hope for the future of man."

T. S. Eliot (1888–1965)

BIBLIOPHILIA AND SAMUEL JOHNSON

"If you wish to have a just notion of the magnitude of this city, you must not be satisfied with seeing its great streets and squares, but must survey the innumerable little lanes and courts. You must visit its quaint, out-of-the-way bookshops, pubs, and tea houses. And of course, you must give estimate to its greatest claim to fame and achievement, the royal collections of the King's Library."
SAMUEL JOHNSON (1709-1784)

He was one of the most important English writers of the eighteenth century. In fact, Samuel Johnson is the single-most-quoted prose writer in the English language in the sundry dictionaries of quotations, and it has long been traditional to refer to the second half of the eighteenth century as the Age of Johnson.

Interestingly though, he is usually remembered not so much as a writer but as a conversationalist and as a personality—mostly due to his biography written by James Boswell in 1791. Indeed, for a long time, thanks largely to a glowing review by Thomas Macaulay in 1831, Boswell's work actually eclipsed Johnson's own writings. Indeed, many of the most famous lines in the quotation dictionaries come not from his works but from his biographer's recollection of his conversation. Boswell has put Johnson in a very small club—authors such as Socrates and Proust—whose most famous works were written by someone else.

Born in Litchfield in 1709, the son of a failed bookseller, Johnson struggled throughout his early life against the ravages of poverty. Although he demonstrated a precocious mind and a prodigious literary talent, he was unable to complete his education at Oxford. Instead he began his lifelong labors as a hack freelance writer in London for a series of newspapers, magazines, journals, and book publishers. He had found comfort and instruction from the books in his father's shop, which prepared him for his role as the century's greatest man of letters. He had received an excellent introduction to classical literature at the Litchfield and Stourbridge Grammar Schools. The combination of his education and his privation enabled him to become phenomenally prolific and adept at virtually every genre—from criticism, translation, poetry, and biography to sermons, parliamentary reports, political polemics, and dramatic stage plays. Although his work was recognized as brilliant, he was never quite able to climb out of the miry privation that seemed to bog him down throughout his life.

At last, when he was nearly fifty, he received a commission to produce a dictionary. Over the course of the next seven years, he single-handedly took on the great task of comprehensively documenting English usage—which, when completed, set the standard for etymology. The work was indeed, stunning. Each word was not only carefully and succinctly defined, but illustrated from classic or poetic literature.

The dictionary earned Dr. Johnson a royal allowance that enabled him to pay off the bill collectors and to live with a modicum of ease. It was during this season of his life that he first met James Boswell, a Scottish ne'er-do-well and spendthrift who had already spent half a lifetime squandering his father's considerable estate on the pleasures of the flesh. Johnson was a pious, thoughtful, bookish, and venerable elder statesman.

As a scholar, albeit a poor scholar, Johnson always depended on public libraries for his reading. He was never able to accumulate a working library of his own when he was young, and by the time he was old he was too set in his ways to begin new habits of study.

Fortunately for him—and for literary posterity—London then had the greatest public library in the world. It was then known as the King's Library—although soon after it would become a part of the British Museum and form the heart of the great British Library.

The museum had been founded about the time Johnson arrived in London. At the time it had only three departments.

The Department of Natural and Artificial Productions developed, in due course, into the antiquities departments of the British Museum. The Department of the Sciences eventually became the Natural History Museum. At first, both of these remained rather meager in resources until well into the nineteenth century. But the Department of Manuscripts and of Printed Books—contained in the King's Library collections—were the most important parts of the original British Museum, and they grew eventually into the greatest library in Britain—perhaps in all the world.

The foundation collection of the library was that of Sir Hans Sloane. This comprised about forty thousand volumes of rare classical works covering the entire spectrum of human achievement. To it was added the royal collection, begun in the time of Henry VII and inherited by George II from his predecessors on the throne.

It was modeled on the ancient library of Alexandria. Numbered among the seven wonders of the ancient world, that library achieved an almost mythic stature in the study of classics from the time of the early Renaissance. The apocryphal burning of the library during Julius Caesar's occupation of the city was often described as the greatest calamity of the ancient world, wherein the most complete collection of all Greek and Near Eastern literature was lost in one great conflagration. In reality, the library and its community of scholars not only flourished during the Hellenistic era of the Ptolemies, but continued to survive throughout the period of the Roman and Byzantine empires. It was not until the capitulation of the Christians of North Africa to the great Moslem Ji'had at the end of the eighth century that the library was destroyed. The great aspiration of King George III was to somehow recover that legendary Alexandrian glory.

By the time Johnson began using the library regularly, the inlaid interleaved copies of the vast catalogue extended to twenty-three volumes. He was thus able to read the greatest books of all time. He imbibed deeply from Aristophanes, Aristotle, Bunyan, Caxton, Cervantes, Chaucer, Cicero, Dante, Dryden, Homer, Horatius Flaccus, Luther, Milton, Ptolemaeus, and Shakespeare as well as from the more contemporaneous Addison, Collins, Hughes, Pope, Parnell, Prior, Pope, Savage, and Watts.

By the time he had begun compiling his dictionary, Johnson was nearly incapacitated with gout, corpulence, and arthritis. By all accounts he was built for the stationary rather than the mobile anyway—overweight and slovenly, asthmatic and awkward. First impressions of him always surprised people. He was big-boned, six feet tall, stout, and stooped. Over a crop of wiry, frizzy hair he wore varying, ill-fitting wigs in unfetching shades of gray. His short-sightedness led to his reading so close to lamps and candles that the wigs frequently bore scorch marks. Today such a man might be held far afield of the priceless books contained in the British Library. But in his own time, he had a remarkable degree of access.

His astonishing acquaintance with the whole range of classical letters is evident in both his dictionary and his prose works. It is what makes his work so compelling, even to this day. But such bibliophilia would have been altogether impossible were it not for the blessing of the public library where he read and studied and worked.

A PRACTICUM ON WORDS

"As he showed the guests round, Dr. Murray would give examples of the unique feature of the Dictionary, the application of the historical method. His task was to trace the life history both of every English word now in use and of all those known to have been in use at any time during the last seven hundred years. His starting point was in 1150, and the early history, variations of sense and form of every word current at that date, was to be given in the same detail as the changes which took place in succeeding centuries. In this he was applying the historical principle much more completely than had been attempted in any country. Although James knew that there would be additions and changes in English vocabulary in future ages, he would stress that, every fact faithfully recorded, and every inference correctly drawn from the facts, becomes a permanent accession to human knowledge part of eternal truth, which will never cease to be true."

K. M. ELISABETH MURRAY (1911–)

Every great library begins in the heart of someone with at least three heroic loves: a love for words, a love for truth, and a love for future generations. Libraries begin as a collection of beloved books, but those books generate a love for words, as well. Perhaps the greatest etymologist of all time was James Murray (1837–1915), a self-educated Scot country boy who was the original editor of the *Oxford English Dictionary*. The fascinating tales of his life and the compilation of the dictionary are told in his granddaughter's own labor of love, *Caught in the Web of Words*, James Murray and the *Oxford English Dictionary*. Murray understood the seed truth about language and the precision inherent in the transferral of truth, first foretold in the biblical story of the Tower of Babel.

We are not all James Murrays, but most readers find themselves quite interested in word studies. These individuals are to be found in the reference sections of bookstores and libraries, lovingly perusing arcane volumes on words such as thesauruses, dictionaries of every sort, encyclopaedias, lists of commonly misspelled words, rhyming dictionaries, and the like. They enjoy language study, especially that of ancient languages, because it lubricates the mind for the various necessary connections etymologists must make—the mental "hooks" upon which to hang word roots and inferences.

We are contemporary, we are busy, we are filled with self-importance and over-value our precious time. But every serious reader will have at their disposal some very good books on words. Here are some of our favorites:

- *The Concise Oxford Dictionary of English Etymology* is a comprehensive guide to word origins.

- *The Merriam-Webster New Book of Word Histories* is less dictionary-like, infused with prose, but somehow not quite as satisfying as the Oxford volume. Still worth owning.
- Beeton's Shilling Dictionaries are wonderful little subject dictionaries published by Ward, Lock, and Co. in the late nineteenth century and early twentieth century. True to our purpose herein, the dictionaries devote quite a bit of space for their compact size to the original meaning and histories of the words they attempt to explain. Samuel and Isabella Beeton are most famous for her *Beeton's Book of Household Management*. After Isabella's untimely young death, Samuel kept control of the publishing company for only a short time. His many imprints were destined to be published by a competitor, Ward, Lock and Co. We own *Beeton's Bible Dictionary*, *Beeton's All About Gardens, Being a Popular Dictionary*, and *Beeton's Dictionary of Universal Information*; comprising geography, history, biography, mythology, Bible knowledge, and chronology, with the pronunciation of every proper name. They were found in English and Scottish bookshops and rejoiced over greatly upon discovery. Original editions of her book on household management have popped up over the years, but, alas, were far too pricey for us to rationalize purchasing when we could possess an albeit new but reasonable paperback copy.

- C. S. Lewis, the masterful novelist, medieval literary scholar, and apologist wrote a wonderful monograph entitled *Studies in Words*. This delectable book is not to be missed.
- Last but not least is Samuel Johnson's own *Dictionary of the English Language*. The predecessor to Murray's great work, it is a marvel of the lexicographer's science and the etymologist's art. In 1755 he undertook the enormous task of compiling his dictionary. While it is often incorrectly called the first English dictionary, it was, nevertheless, the most important dictionary—indeed, it was the dictionary until Murray's *Oxford English Dictionary* appeared a century and a half later. We still find it to be enormously useful and keep a modern abridged edition right beside our writing desk.

Literary Pursuits

*B*rowsing is but one of the many time-honored traditions
that have been heedlessly cast aside amid the hustle and bustle
of modernity. Nevertheless, it is a habit that seems almost as
natural as breathing in a bookstore. Whether it is a fine old
antiquarian dealer with dusty shelves, dark labyrinthine
rooms, and hidden treasures in every stack or a familiar
neighborhood shop featuring fresh coffee, warm conversations,
and the latest bestsellers, readers relish the comfortable haunts
of their determined hunts nearly as much as they love the
books they ultimately find there.

"Where is human nature so weak as in the bookstore?"
Henry Ward Beecher (1813–1887)

"If a book is worth reading, it is worth buying."
John Ruskin (1819–1900)

"When I get a little money, I buy books; and if there is any left, I buy food and clothes."
Desiderius Erasmus (1466–1536)

"A bookststore is an earthly elysium. In some strange way, it seems to represent so much of what man aspires to and it embodies so much of what man yearns for. Like a well-stocked library, a good used bookstore can be a sort of nexus of piety and sensuality, of holiness and seduction. Such sanctuaries from the hustle bustle of everyday life are in some sense cenacles of virtue, vessels of erudition, arks of prudence, towers of wisdom, domains of meekness, bastions of strength, and thuribles of sanctity as well as crucibles of dissipation, throne rooms of desire, caryatids of opulence, repositories of salaciousness, milieus of concupiscence, and trusses of extravagance."

ɘ{ *Tristan Gylberd (1954–)* }ɘ

"When you sell a man a book you don't sell him just twelve ounces of paper and ink and glue—you sell him a whole new life. Love and friendship and humor and ships at sea by night—there's all heaven and earth in a book, a real book I mean."

ɘ{ *Christopher Morley (1890–1957)* }ɘ

"Bookselling is the most ticklish and unsafe and hazardous of all professions scarcely with the exception of horse jockeyship."
Walter Scott (1771–1832)

"When I am dead
I hope it will be said:
His sins were scarlet,
But his books were read."
Hilaire Belloc (1870–1953)

"I love the smell of book ink in the morning."
Umberto Eco (1929–)

"New York, Paris, London, Vienna, Prague, Edinburgh, Milan, and Amsterdam, aside from all their obvious attractions, are great cities because they are book cities."
◦ꝗ Henry van Dyke (1853–1933) ꝗ◦

"There is a class of street-readers, whom I never contemplate without affection—the poor gentry, who, not having the where-withal to buy or hire a book, filch a little learning at the open stalls—the owner, with his hard eye, casting envious looks at them all the while, and thinking when they will have done. Venturing tenderly, page after page, expecting every moment he shall interpose his interdict, and yet unable to deny themselves the gratification, they snatch a fearful joy."
◦ꝗ Charles Lamb (1775–1834) ꝗ◦

"The creative arts consist of signs. Thus, if images are, as Aristotle long ago asserted, the literature of the layman, then books consist of signs of signs. And thus, bookshops consist of signs of signs of signs. They are thus, the truest of all the creative arts—combining rhythm, tone, structure, progression, logic, melody, heft, texture, redolence, cipher, perspective, harmony, balance, epic, symbol, emblem, saga, craftsmanship, hue, lyric, form, function, ballad, and sanctity. They are united in their variety and varied in their unity, unique in their diversity and diverse in their apt assembly. They are sustained by a law at once heavenly and worldly. The rich fragrance of hand-oiled Moroccan leathers, the visual panoply of deep natural hues, the effluvium of fine vellum, the hollow ring of sequestered silence, the sacred spectacle of light filtered through high dusty windows, and the hush of monkish thoughtfulness combine to grant fine antiquarian bookstores an air of amplitude. The total effect is of a concert of alluring terrestrial beauty and majestic supernatural signals."

Tristan Gylberd (1954–)

"By Charing Cross in London Town
There runs a road of high renown,
Where antique books are ranged on shelves
As dark and dusty as themselves.
And many book lovers have spent
Their substance there with great content,
And vexed their wives and filled their homes
With faded prints and massive tomes."
Norman Davey (1888–1959)

"It is a good plan to have a book with you in all places and at
all times. If you are presently without, hurry without delay to
the nearest shop and buy one of mine."
Oliver Wendell Holmes (1809–1894)

"A bookstore is like a treasure house, storing up all the wisdom of the ages, all the adventures of a lifetime, and all the sensual delights of the moment, for it is in a bookstore that all the shared experiences of literate man are assembled and disseminated for all who have eyes to see, ears to hear, and minds to conceive."

Italo Calvino (1923–1985)

"There is no greater delight for an author than to stumble upon a copy of one of his own books in an unfamiliar book-shop. Of course, the comfort and consolation is soon dissi-pated when he discovers, to his dismay, that he has far more books in hand to purchase that he can ever hope to sell in that little place."

Tristan Gylberd (1954–)

TOOLS AND CHARLES SPURGEON

"My books are my tools. They also serve as my counsel, my consolation, and my comfort. They are my source of wisdom and the font of my education. They are my friends and my delights. They are my surety, when all else is awry, that I have set my confidence in the substantial things of truth and right."
CHARLES SPURGEON (1834–1892)

Even though he was best known as a world-renowned author, preacher, and philanthropist, the bookshops of London knew Charles Spurgeon as a voracious reader and an avid collector.

He was the nineteenth century's most famous clergyman in the world. In 1854, just four years after his conversion, Charles Spurgeon, then just barely twenty years old, became pastor of London's famed New Park Street Church—formerly pastored by the famous Puritans John Gill and John Rippon. The young preacher was an immediate success. The congregation quickly outgrew their building, moved to Exeter Hall, then to Surrey Music Hall. In these venues Spurgeon frequently preached to audiences numbering in the tens of thousands—all in the days before electronic amplification. In 1861 the congregation moved permanently to the newly constructed Metropolitan Tabernacle. It quickly became the largest congregation in the world.

When he arrived in London, there were just over two hundred members in the congregation. Nearly forty years later, after his lifetime of labor, the number had increased to nearly six thousand. With his rhetorical passion, literary eloquence, and stalwart orthodoxy, Spurgeon regularly drew standing-room-only crowds—which included the likes of Prime Minister William Gladstone, Lord Chief Justice Campbell, Earl Grey, the Lord Mayor and Sheriffs of London, Earl Russell, Lord Alfred Paget, Lord Panmure, Earl Shaftesbury, the Duchess of Sutherland, Florence Nightingale, Dr. Livingstone, several members of the royal family, innumerable members of Parliament, as well as throngs of the common folk of London—to both the Sunday and weekday services at the church.

His popularity caused great demand for his printed sermons that circulated in almost countless volumes. In one year a quarter of a million copies of his sermon tracts were distributed in the colleges of Oxford and Cambridge. A number of prominent American newspapers printed the sermons every week and called him the greatest preacher of the age. Over the years Spurgeon published nearly four thousand sermons and more than a hundred books on a wide variety of subjects.

He was also the founder of more than sixty philanthropic institutions including orphanages, colporterage societies, schools, colleges, clinics, and hospitals. In addition he established more than twenty mission churches and dozens of Sunday and Ragged Schools throughout England.

But in the midst of the busyness of his life and ministry, he always found time to read. Books were his most constant companions, and bookstores were his most regular haunts.

Spurgeon was born in 1834 in the little Essex village of Kelvedon. Both his father and grandfather were pastors, and so he was raised around books, reading, and piety. As a youngster he began a lifelong habit of diligent and unending reading—typically, he read six books per week, and he was able to remember what he had read and where he had read it many years later. He particularly loved old books. He claimed in his autobiography that before he was ten years old, he preferred to go into his grandfather's study and pull down an old Puritan classic and read rather than go outside and play with friends.

As he grew older, his passion for books and the little shops that sold them remained unabated. Each day Spurgeon would scour the newspapers to find when an antiquarian bookshop might be selling certain books. He would then beat a hasty path to the shop to purchase the treasure—or if he was too busy that day with appointments, he would send his secretary to buy the book. In time his personal library numbered more than twelve thousand volumes.

The books were all shelved in Spurgeon's study at Westwood, his family home. The oldest book in the collection was a commentary on the Book of Psalms by the infamous inquistor, Cardinal Juan de Torquemada (1482–1531). Written in Latin and published in Rome in 1476, Spurgeon found it on the bottom shelf of one of his favorite bookshops just off the Royal Mile in Edinburgh. He acquired a magnificent set of the complete works of Thomas Chalmers—signed, numbered, and in mint condition. He also had rare copies of the commentaries by Matthew Henry, John Calvin, Adam Clarke, Robert Jamieson, Isaac Williams, and Nicholas Byfield. The hymns of Isaac Watts and the compilations of John Rippon and Samuel, John, and Charles Wesley were also collected by him—resulting in an outstanding accumulation of hymns written between the seventeenth and nineteenth centuries.

Of course, Spurgeon was not merely a collector. He was utilitarian, if anything. He viewed his books as the tools of his trade. And the shops where he found them were essentially his hardware stores. As a result, the books were used. They were hardly museum pieces, despite their scarcity or value. They were the natural extensions of his work and ministry.

The great library he collected over his lifetime was kept intact after his death in 1892. Mrs. Spurgeon wanted to retain the library as a memorial to her husband. She hoped ultimately to have both Westwood and the library there turned into a kind of museum. But when she died in 1903, their twin sons, Thomas and Charles, decided that not only did they have to sell the home but they also had to sell the larger part of their father's library. The idea of a museum dedicated to their father seemed financially unfeasible at the time.

They advertised in English newspapers that the books were for sale. Amazingly, the library stood for sale for more than two years. Books had to be sold off piecemeal. Eventually, many of the rarest volumes were sold off to individual investors. At last, in 1905, a trustee of William Jewell College secured the remaining five thousand volumes for the little Baptist college in rural Missouri—where it remains to this day, displayed in a vaulted replica of Spurgeon's Westwood study built by the Carnegie Foundation. At last, Spurgeon's museum—a tribute to a ministry, to a love for books, and to a passion for bookshops—stands half a world away from where the great man lived and worked and read.

A PRACTICUM ON BOOKSHOPS

*"The smaller, the odder, the more out of the way, and the more special-
ized, the better. That is my philosophy on bookshops. Come to think of
it, that is my philosophy on everything else too—it makes for a very
interesting life unconstrained by the smothering expectations of the
tyranny of fashion or popularity."*
TRISTAN GYLBERD (1954–)

We twirled a lot," sighs Meg Ryan's darling character in reply to
Tom Hanks's character's query about the photograph of a small
twirling child and her mother over Ryan's shoulder. In *You've Got
Mail*, Hanks's evil chain bookstore empire is poised to put Ryan's
quaint little second-generation bookshop out of business. Later, as
Ryan is locking her shop's door for the last time, in memory's eye
she sees the living image of the two twirling figures, love and
imagination, future promise and laughter swirling around them
like twinkling sprites and fairies. The effect is magical. One simply
cannot conjure up such a scene in the evil chain store empire
across the street, where workers don't know anything about the
books available in their subject area and homey touches are
replaced by steel, glass, and gourmet coffee. Meg and Tom are the

engaging stars of the film, but the moviemakers knew well that to audiences everywhere, the demise of Ryan's bookshop would hit home in a wave of nostalgia and would position the sympathetic character perfectly.

Small bookshops barely hang on in the shadows of large chains, but of course their plight is no different from that of small groceries, hardware stores, and other vestiges of local community. This is no longer an American phenomenon; it is a global one.

Happily, used and antiquarian bookstores continue to lurch right along. Megaliths simply cannot function profitably in the individualistic atmosphere of used books. Sorting and cataloging the varied titles and condition of antiquarian books cannot be performed on a grand scale profitably. Oh, there are some large stores trafficking in remaindered books (publishers' overstocks sold in bulk to retailers). They are not to be confused with the stores worth patronizing that deal in old books. These friends are to be found in almost every town and certainly each city. From Edinburgh to Houston to New York, we have favorite shops which sell forgotten books.

We are careful to avoid those places that stay in business fueled mostly by the rapid circulation of paperback romance titles. Instead, we search out those slightly dusty places—at least one sneeze is de rigueur upon entering—where the loves of the owners are displayed in varied subject areas hand-labeled "Gardening," "Civil War," "English Poetry 1700s," "Natural History," "Art, Watercolor," "Biography," and "Geography." A great store is defined by the personality of the owner who invariably presides over a desk with stacks of books almost obscuring his or her face, glasses perched on nose so that you are peered at from an angle, and who knows exactly which book you are describing and where it rests upon the brimming shelves of his or her small kingdom. Do not confuse these shops with those full of used technical books and those with no heart. Knowing the difference between a book-store with heart and one which is dry and uninspiring is a lot like babies' cries: to know the difference between a mad cry and a hungry cry, a tired one and the one that screams, "Drop every-thing and run to me now; Charissa is using the plunger on my face!" takes practice. It takes time spent together, getting to know one another, and no one can really teach you the difference. One day you hear the cry and don't rush to the infant. You hear your-self say, "Oh, he's just fussy," and you finish stirring the soup before you retrieve the mewling prince. Or in the case of a book-store, "Oh, let's not spend any time here, he doesn't have any-thing," even though you're standing in a catacomb of books.

Ah, but there is another category which exists in even more rarified dust-laden air. There exists in the bookish chain of

being a higher order of bookshop just this side of the "lost hori-
zon." There is that rarest of places, a shop in the home of a
committed collector whose love for a subject or someone's body
of work forces them to snatch up available good copies to preserve them for others who are serious about carrying on the
particular traditions of knowledge and ideas. Such a shop exists
in a small town in the Thames Valley, near Oxford, and it is
everything the collector could ever ask for. The owner has collected pieces from the homes of two of our favorite writers and
will serve tea while we peruse carefully collected books,
sketches, and other touchstones available for purchase. Here is
the bookshop with true heart, the once-in-a-lifetime place
inhabited by the kindred spirit who is immediately beloved
upon making acquaintance.

We could twirl there.

- Whenever possible, order new books from local bookshops.
  Just because the book is not in stock doesn't mean it can't be
  ordered and available within a week. Use chain stores when
  your bookshop can't provide service and as a place to see what
  new stuff is available and for magazines.
- What subjects interest you? Begin looking in local used bookshops in just those areas to learn their stock.

- Just because a book is old and leatherbound and in great shape doesn't mean you have to buy it. If no one reads it, it is only taking up precious space. Save your money for the books of your dreams.
- Does the bookstore owner seem friendly and interested? He or she might be a curmudgeon, but a good bookstore's owner can be roused when he or she ascertains that you are seriously looking for something. Do not be demanding, but inquisitive. If the owner is absentmindedly tapping away at a computer or reading and refuses to stir in response to your honest questions, leave quickly and shake the dust off your feet. Better books await you elsewhere. The manner of the owner reflects the enthusiasm and knowledge with which books for the shop are selected.
- When you arrive in a new place and have time for bookshop visits, look in the Yellow Pages and begin to make calls. When you find a good shop, ask for their recommendations for other good shops in the area. This is your best resource. Don't bother asking at worthless shops. The vacant stare they will give you reflects their fear of competition, not lack of understanding of your question.
- You must frequent good shops because their stock fluctuates. If you don't find anything you're searching for one day, you might find ten books on the next visit. Once you become a

frequent customer, the owner might even call you when something comes in that he or she knows would interest you.

- High prices don't necessarily denote rarity. Some owners over-value their books. Keep looking. On the other hand, if you find the book of your dreams, buy it. As with any antique, it might not be there when you return.

- When travelling, ask your local bookshop owners if they can recommend good shops in the region of your destination.

- If you are still intent on pursuing the bigger-is-better dream, try visiting the Strand. One of the world's largest bookstores, this vast cornucopia of all things bookish is the place where the Bass family has served the needs of literary New Yorkers since 1929. Featuring more than two million books on eight miles of shelves in a thirty-two-thousand-square-foot space on four floors, the Strand makes the modern Barnes and Noble or Borders megastores look downright dinky. It is the sort of place where we find that we can wander—or twirl—for hours from section to section completely agog at the range of the selection.

Literary Things

*O*ne thing leads to another. Once a person begins the journey
toward a literate and literary life, he finds that he has not only
begun to collect old books, haunt antiquarian shops, and
rearrange the décor of his home to maximize reading spaces, he
has also begun to collect odd bookshelves, functional side tables,
elaborate notebooks, leather journals, parchment papers, old
maps, bottles of ink, eccentric blotters, and tortoise shell fountain pens. It is not just that an attachment to Victorian accou-
trements and ephemera seem apt for the inquisitive life, it is
that a taste for finer, more substantial things, breeds a taste for
more in kind. Serious reading all too often entails serious tools.

"The creative mind plays with the objects it loves."
Carl Jung (1875–1961)

"Books, books, books. It was not that I read and reread the same ones. But all of them were necessary to me. Their presence, their smell, the letters of their titles, and the texture of their leather bindings. And then there are all the things that go with the books: the fine papers, the funny little tables, the comfortable chairs, the pens made for slow and reflective writing. It is all a beautiful and enticing culture, is it not?"
Camilla Colette (1813–1895)

"Style is the dress of thoughts. The implements we surround ourselves with are the outward manifestation of the inward array."
Lord Chesterfield (1694–1773)

"If the crowns of all the kingdoms of
Europe were laid down at my feet
In exchange for my books and things
And my great love of reading,
I would, assuredly, spurn them all."

&ngn; *Francois Fenelon (1651–1715)* &ngn;

"A busy man's life is generally one prolonged effort to avoid
reading in order to prevent thinking. The accumulated stuff
of his life distracts him from anything worthwhile. The
thoughtful reader, on the other hand, surrounds himself with
inducements to substance."

&ngn; *Aldous Huxley (1894–1963)* &ngn;

"When we say that culture is to know the best that has been
thought and said in the world, we imply that, for culture, a
system directly tending toward this end is necessary in our
reading and our collecting of those things which induce our
reading."

&ngn; *Matthew Arnold (1822–1888)* &ngn;

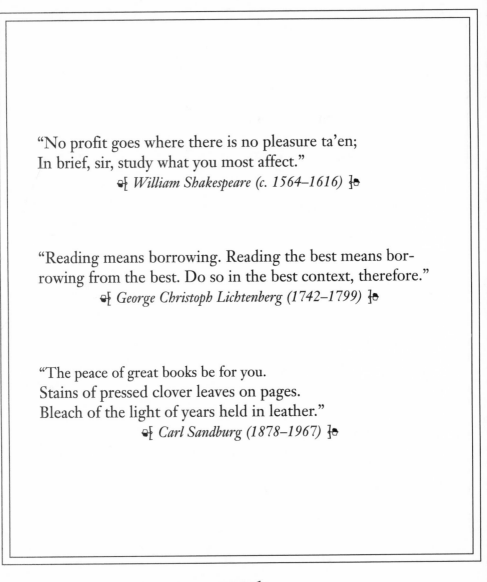

"No profit goes where there is no pleasure ta'en;
In brief, sir, study what you most affect."
        ❧ *William Shakespeare (c. 1564–1616)* ❧

"Reading means borrowing. Reading the best means borrowing from the best. Do so in the best context, therefore."
        ❧ *George Christoph Lichtenberg (1742–1799)* ❧

"The peace of great books be for you.
Stains of pressed clover leaves on pages.
Bleach of the light of years held in leather."
        ❧ *Carl Sandburg (1878–1967)* ❧

"That is a part of the beauty of all literature. You discover that your longings are universal longings, that you're not alive and isolated from anyone. You belong. The literary environment then ought to be a manifestation of that commonality, that community with full and tangible reminders in the very decor."

F. Scott Fitzgerald (1896–1940)

"Of all the inanimate objects, of all men's creations, books are the nearest to us, for they contain our very thoughts, our ambitions, our indignations, our illusions, our fidelity to truth, and our persistent leaning toward error. But most of all they resemble us in the precarious hold on life. They ought to be accompanied by the objects by which men create them—so that their truest nature may be manifest for all to sense assure."

Joseph Conrad (1857–1924)

"Books we know,
Are a substantial world,
Both pure and good.
Round which, with tendrils
Strong as flesh and blood,
Our pastimes and our happiness
Will grow."

William Wordsworth (1770–1850)

"The way a book is read—which is to say, the qualities a
reader brings to a book—can have as much to do with its
worth as anything the author puts into it. Anyone who can
read can learn how to read deeply and thus live more fully."

Martin Galbreth (1922–1998)

"Things have hardly changed since the primordial days of prehistory. We are just as apt to settle to read any work of fiction with a squirm of anticipation as the most distant primitive people might have experienced as they gathered closer to the fire and the storyteller began the tale. Ought we not then prepare the site of our intellectual bonfire with the same great care and attention to detail as they did in the long ago and far away?"

❧ *Peter de Vries (1910–1993)* ☙

"I own that I am disposed to say grace upon twenty other occasions in the course of the day besides my dinner; why have we none for books?"

Charles Lamb (1775–1834)

"As imagination bodies forth
The forms of things unknown, the poet's pen
Turns them to shapes, and gives to airy nothing
A local habitation and a name."

William Shakespeare (c. 1564–1616)

E PHEMERA AND THEODORE ROOSEVELT

*"At Sagamore Hill we love a great many things—birds and trees and books
and all things beautiful, children and gardens and hard work and the joy of
life. The place puts me in the mood for a good story. Of course, I am always
in the mood for a good story. Perhaps that is why I am rather more apt to
read old books than new ones. And perhaps that is why I surround myself
with reminders of stories, long ago told, or those yet to be told. Life ought to
be redolent with the stuff of life from which the stories of life inevitably
spring."*
THEODORE ROOSEVELT (1858-1919)

H e was a voracious learner and an avid reader throughout his
extraordinary life. It is hard to imagine though, when he might have
found the time. Before his fiftieth birthday he had served as a New
York State legislator, the under-secretary of the navy, police commissioner for the City of New York, U.S. Civil Service commissioner, the governor of New York, the U.S. vice president under
William McKinley, a colonel in the U.S. Army, and two terms as the
president of the United States. In addition, he had run a cattle
ranch in the Dakota Territories, served as a reporter and editor for
several journals, newspapers, and magazines, and conducted scientific expeditions on four continents. He wrote nearly fifty books on

an astonishing array of subjects—from history and biography to natural science and social criticism.

He enjoyed hunting, boxing, and wrestling. He was an amateur taxidermist, botanist, ornithologist, and astronomer. He was a devoted family man who lovingly raised six children. And he enjoyed a lifelong romance with his wife.

How he possibly squeezed reading into the crowded hours of his life was a matter of some substantial speculation among those who observed him flash across the stage of history.

Among his friends he counted the greatest writers, thinkers, scholars, and scientists of his day. And by all accounts he was the best read of them all—being readily conversant on everything from the traditional classics to the most recent philosophical, sociological, or technological musings. He usually read at least five books a week—unless he wasn't too busy, in which case, he read more. And yet his attitude toward the torrid pace of his intellectual pursuit was refreshingly relaxed: "I am old-fashioned, or sentimental, or something about books. Whenever I read one I want, in the first place, to enjoy myself, and, in the next place, to feel that I am a little better and not a little worse for having read it."

His son Quentin claimed that he read every book received at the Library of Congress—which, of course, he surely did not. But many of his friends testified that however new the volume they recommended to him, he had always read it already. "His range of reading is amazing," wrote the science fiction writer H. G. Wells. "He seems to be echoing with all the thought of the time, and he has receptivity to the pitch of genius." Guglielmo Marconi, the great Italian physicist and inventor, was amazed by his knowledge in the specialized field of Italian history and literature. "That man actually cited book after book that I've never heard of, much less read. He's going to keep me busy for some time just following his Italian reading." And the English diplomat, Lord Charnwood, asserted, "No statesman for centuries has had his width of intellectual range."

As a result of his relentless studies and his near-perfect recall, Roosevelt's knowledge was highly integrated, and he was continually crossing boundaries, moving back and forth from one area of human knowledge to another. He was thus able to make connections that mere specialists were unable to make.

According to Viscount Lee, "Whether the subject of the moment was political economy, the Greek drama, tropical fauna or flora, the Irish sagas, protective coloration in nature, metaphysics, the technique of football, or postfuturist painting, he was equally at home with the experts and drew out the best that was in them." Indeed, "In one afternoon," said his son Archie, "I have heard him speak to the foremost Bible student of the world, a prominent ornithologist, an Asian diplomat, and a French general, all of whom agreed that Father knew more about the subjects on which they had specialized than they did."

Indeed, his mind was omnivorous and his interests were dizzying. "Can you come for dinner either Wednesday or Friday?" he wrote to Henry Cabot Lodge's wife. "Then we could discuss the Hittite Empire, the Pithecanthropus, Magyar love songs, the exact relations of the Atli of the Volsunga Saga to the Etzel of the Nibelungenlied, and both to Attila—with interludes about the rate bill, Beveridge, and other matters of more vivid contemporary interest."

But for all his prodigious knowledge, he was supremely unpretentious. All he ever claimed for himself was zest—"delight in the play of the mind for its own sake." But others were rather more impressed. The famed academic Vilhjalmur Stefansson asserted, "It is to be supposed, seeing that Roosevelt is human, that there must be some fields in which he is ill-informed, but none of these have ever come to my attention, nor, so far as I know, to the attention of any of my friends in the various spheres of scientific or cultural exploration."

"If you want to lead, you must read" was a maxim that Roosevelt took seriously. It was merely an extension of his whole philosophy of life: Making the most of his mind was of a piece with making the most of his body. It was merely an exercise of good stewardship.

His Long Island home, Sagamore Hill, was always filled with books. But it was filled with much more—all the things that he called the "ephemera of the literary life." Like Ulysses, he had seen all the wonders of the world. He traveled extensively throughout North America, Europe, Africa, the Middle East, and Central and South America. He enjoyed his stays amid the hustle and bustle of the world's greatest cities. And he relished his opportunities to tramp about in the world's most untamed wildernesses. But his lifelong conviction was that for all the majesty, splendor, mystery of those distant realms, there was no place like home.

He designed, built, and filled Sagamore Hill. It was a spacious, old-fashioned house surrounded by wide porches overlooking Oyster Bay and punctuated with a bevy of large fireplaces. Its shingled exterior was notable for its profusion of gables and chimneys, while the interior boasted large rooms with high ceilings, dark Edwardian furnishings, and dozens of hunting trophies in every available nook and cranny.

In every way the house reflected the personality of the larger-than-life family that occupied it. The great New York photojournalist, Jacob Riis, testified that it "fairly shouted the vim, vigor, and vitality of its proprietors."

Like most avid readers, Roosevelt loved to collect things. He loved ornate fountain pens, leather writing journals, and wooden boxes. He gathered about him reminders of great stories, favorite writers, and principal heroes. His desk was cluttered with statuary, photographs, and a mad accumulation of mementos.

He had set aside one of the upstairs sleeping porches specifically for Bible reading and Bible study—which had always been a vital part of his daily life. "A thorough knowledge of the Bible," he argued, "is worth more than a college education." The reason for this was not simply that the Bible outlined a good and acceptable system of personal morals and social etiquette. He believed that the Bible was far more than that—it was, in fact, the very warp and woof of the fabric of western civilization. It was therefore an essential element of the maintenance of order, civility, and prosperity. Indeed, without it, the great American experiment in liberty would be thrown into very real jeopardy. "Every thinking man, when he thinks, realizes that the teachings of the Bible are so interwoven and entwined with our whole civic and social life that it would be literally impossible for us to figure ourselves what that life would be if these standards were removed. We would lose almost all the standards by which we now judge both public and private morals; all the standards which we, with more or less resolution, strive to raise ourselves."

He quoted the Bible often—evincing his intimate familiarity with it. One biographical archivist examined just his published works and found that he had so integrated Scripture into his thought processes that there were actually more than forty-two hundred biblical images, references, inferences, or complete quotations contained therein. And his unpublished letters, articles, and speeches contained hundreds—perhaps even thousands—more. On that little porch at Sagamore Hill, he collected the ephemera necessary for serious Bible study—maps, concordances, marking pens, and notebooks as well as a small framed collection of the famous Holy Land watercolors of David Roberts.

Often, Roosevelt would spend hours sitting on the front porch simply reading and rocking. Of course, for him, simply reading and rocking took on a whole new definition: He rocked his chair so vigorously that it would traverse the entire length of the porch while so immersed in his book that he never noticed. His wife Edith often scolded him for his hyperactivity. He just replied, "You relax your way, I'll relax mine."

At the end of his life, he took special comfort in his home—and all his bits of literary ephemera. Tired from his many battles, enfeebled by his injuries and illnesses, and frustrated by the foolhardiness of the current political scene, Roosevelt often retreated to his library and porches to think, reflect, convalesce, and rest. The night he died, his final words to Edith were, "I wonder if you will ever know how I love Sagamore Hill."

How could he not? He had made it after his own image. He had gathered there all his favorite things. He had built his extraordinary life upon its foundations.

And after all, there is no place like home.

A Practicum on Stacks

"The majority, though they are sometimes frequent readers, do not set much store by reading. They turn to it as a last resource. They abandon it with alacrity as soon as any alternative pastime turns up. It is kept for railway journeys, illnesses, odd moments of enforced solitude, or for the process called reading oneself to sleep. They sometimes combine it with desultory conversation; often, with listening to the radio. But literary people are always looking for leisure and silence in which to read and do so with their whole attention. When they are denied such attentive and undisturbed reading even for a few days they feel impoverished."
C. S. Lewis (1898-1963)

Reading is not a "hobby." It is a lifestyle of learning! When someone describes their hobbies as reading, collecting Meissen porcelain angels, and playing darts, it is a tiny, if fallible, indication that they read only on vacation and when they "have time."

True readers are curious above all things. They read about their hobbies, which may be bird watching, skeet, genealogy, or leaf mold patterns in Victorian naturalist sketches—see Beatrix Potter's early work. A reader reads cereal boxes, vitamin bottle labels, subway advertisements, newspapers, Internet resources,

CD inserts, magazines, soap and shampoo bottles (especially Dr. Bronner's infamous peppermint oil soap), catalog copy, and all manner of the printed word besides books. Books are a given; other reading is the ganglia of the voracious curiosity inherent in a true Reader.

Find a Reader, and you have found the source of stacks. Neat or messy in personal habit, outgoing backslapper or bespectacled introvert of the most stereotypical sort, every true Reader is also a stacker. Beside the bed, beside the favorite reading spot, tucked away in the car, on top of the day planner notebook, on top of shelves and underneath photo frames, are stacks of books.

Stacks can be classified variously. There are stacks of books that simply must be read next. There are stacks of books one should read, but never get around to. They are composed of gift books from well-meaning nonreaders. There are stacks of books about current areas of interest. There are stacks of books one is readying to use for study. There are stacks of books in the formation period upon discovering a new interest. There are stacks of books so beautiful they cannot be hidden. There are stacks of books referred to as often as once a day. It's possible even that the works of those who have returned to the dust of the earth now reside under the dust of their authors. See the chapter on literary pursuits and antiquarian bookstores—re: dust.

What can be done with stacks that the reader would rather
not, cannot, most assuredly will not re-shelve?

- Place lovingly in the den as decoration or on the coffee table.
- Buy several small decorative shelves and place small stacks on
  these shelves hung about the house.
- Above all, treat these stacks lovingly and as single units, for
  the Reader will confuse them with part of his or her own mind
  and spirit.
- Use them as display bases for related arcane collections: i.e. pen
  sets atop books on pens or letter-writing, journals atop favorite
  author biographies or books on writing . . . You get the idea.
- Consider the purchase of *The National Trust Manual of House-
  keeping*, a most useful guide on the conservation of old houses
  and their contents. Where else would one find an entire chapter on the care of books and documents? It also gives due
  treatment to the care of various collections. Page 181 of the
  1993 edition includes a photograph of boxing squirrels to
  illustrate the cleaning of mammal specimens in the chapter
  entitled "Natural History Collections."

Literary Associations

A wide variety of people, places, or things may be able to conjure up literary associations for us—our reading friends, the homes of our favorite writers, or locales connected with a vivid scene that has remained in our mind's eye many years after we first observed it on the pages of a book. These associations are as vital an aspect of the shelf life as are the books, the legends, the stories, and the experiences themselves—just as they always have been; just as they always will be.

"Now a congenial book can be taken up by any lover of books, with the certainty of its transporting the reader within a few minutes to a region immeasurably removed from that which he desires to quit. The shape or pattern of the magic carpet whereon he flies through space and time is of no consequence. The son of science is rapt by a problem; the philosopher by an abstruse speculation; the antiquary is carried centuries back into the chivalric past; the lover of poetry is borne upon glittering wings into the future. The charm works well for all. Books are the blessed unction of the mind."

James Payn (1830–1898)

"The student has his Rome, his Florence, his whole glowing Italy, within the four walls of his own library. He has in his books the ruins of an antique world, and the glories of a modern one."

Henry Wadsworth Longfellow (1807–1882)

"The reading of all good books is like a conversation with the finest men of past centuries."

Rene Descartes (1596–1650)

"A good writer is basically a story-teller, not a scholar or a redeemer of mankind."
Isaac Bashevis Singer (1904–1991)

"The reason why so few good books are written is that so few people who can write know anything."
Walter Bagehot (1826–1877)

"A poem is never finished, only abandoned."
Paul Valery (1871–1945)

"Misspending a man's time is a kind of self-homicide."
Marquess de Halifax (1633–1695)

"There are but four sorts or readers. First, there are sponges that suck up everything and, when pressed give it out in the same state, only perhaps somewhat dirtier. Second, there are the sand glasses—or rather the upper half of the sand glass, which in a brief hour assuredly lets out what it has received—and whose reading is only a profitless measurement and dozing away of time. Third, there are straining bags who get rid of whatever is good and pure, and retain the dregs. And this class is again subdivided into species of the sensual, who retain evil for gratification of their own base imagination, and the calumnious, who judge only by defects, and to whose envy a beauty is an eyesore, a fervent praise respecting a near-grievance, and the more virulent in its action because the miserable man does not dare confess the truth to his own heart. Fourth, and lastly, there are the great moguls—diamond sieves—which is perhaps going farther for a smile than its superior dignity can repay, inasmuch as a common colander would have been equally symbolic, but imperial or culinary, these are the only good, and I fear the least numerous, who assuredly gain the good, while the superfluous or impure passes away and leaves no trace."

Samuel Taylor Coleridge (1772–1834)

"Often have I sighed to measure
By myself a lonely pleasure
Sighed to think I read a book
Only read, perhaps, by me."
⊰ *William Wordsworth (1770–1850)* ⊱

"Books are not dead things but do contain a potency of life
in them to be as active as that soul was whose progeny they
are; nay, they do preserve as in a vial the purest extraction of
that living intellect that bred them."
⊰ *John Milton (1608–1674)* ⊱

"A book is good company. It comes to your longing with full
instruction, but pursues you never. It is not offended at your
absent-mindedness, nor jealous if you turn to other pleasures,
of leaf, or dress, or mineral, or even of books. It silently serves
the soul without recompense, not even for the hire of love.
And yet more noble, it seems to pass from itself, and to enter
the memory, and to hover in a silvery transformation there,
until the outward book is but a body and its soul and spirit are
flown to you, and possess your memory like a spirit."
⊰ *Henry Ward Beecher (1813–1887)* ⊱

"Every book is, in an intimate sense, a circular letter to the friends of him who writes it."

Robert Louis Stevenson (1850-1894)

"A man's needs are few. The simpler the life, therefore, the better. Indeed, only three things are truly necessary in order to make life happy: the blessing of God, the benefit of books, and the benevolence of friends."

Thomas Chalmers (1780–1847)

"At the hazard of losing some credit on this head, I must confess that I dedicate no inconsiderable portion of my time to other people's thoughts. I dream away my life in others' speculations. I love to lose myself in other men's minds. When I am not walking, I am reading; I cannot sit and think. Books think for me."

Charles Lamb (1775–1834)

"All kinds of things rejoiced my soul in the company of my friends—to talk and laugh and do each other kindnesses; read pleasant books together, pass from lightest jesting to talk of the deepest things and back again; differ without rancour, as a man might differ with himself, and when most rarely dissension arose find our normal agreement all the sweeter for it; teach each other or learn from each other; be impatient for the return of the absent, and welcome them with joy on their homecoming; these and such like things, proceeding from our hearts as we gave affection and received it back, and shown by face, by voice, by the eyes, and a thousand other pleasing ways, kindled a flame which infused our very souls and of many made us one. This is what men value in friends."
St. Augustine (354–430)

"I am persuaded both children and the lower class of readers hate books which are written down to their capacity and love those that are more composed for their elders and betters."
Walter Scott (1771–1832)

CREATIVITY AND MARK TWAIN

"Creativity is even more difficult a thing to stimulate and sustain than love—though it is pursued with the same regularity and rigor."
MARK TWAIN (1835-1910)

At the turn of the century, the great American satirist, journalist, and novelist Mark Twain called the cosmopolitan New England city of Hartford his home. He once quipped, "Of all the beautiful towns it has been my fortune to see, this is the chief." Most people probably think he was looking out over the wide twists and slow turns of the muddy Mississippi as he wrote his most popular books. In fact, he wrote a good number of them while looking out over the Park River there in central Connecticut.

Today, Hartford, located midway between New York and Boston, is the capital of the Connecticut. The city is a center of government and a wide range of commercial, social, and cultural activities. But it is perhaps best known as the Insurance Capital of the World. Aetna, CIGNA, ITT Hartford, Phoenix Mutual, and Travelers are some of the larger insurance firms that make their corporate headquarters in Hartford.

When Twain lived and worked there, Hartford was more of an artist's colony than anything else—home to such luminaries as Louisa May Alcott, Harriet Beecher Stowe, and William Dean Howells.

In 1871, having already gained publishing success with his book *Innocents Abroad*, Twain decided to move to this quaint town so full of literary associations. This was so he might devote himself entirely to writing fiction. He hired architect Edward Tuckerman Potter to erect for him a palace of creativity.

The result was a wonderfully colorful brick Victorian mansion complete with a massive library and a billiard room that boasted spectacular views from tall turreted windows. The house was regally ornamented with geometrical motifs, and it featured towers, turrets, chimneys, balconies, a covered veranda, and a porte cochere. In this facinating pastiche, a picturesque notion of a medieval bastion was combined with the attenuated lines of a Gothic cathedral and the fussy kitsch of a cuckoo clock.

Twain loved it. He loved the way the architecture bespoke creativity. He loved the stimulation of literary friends and a literary social life. He loved the bucolic New England culture with all its connections to Mather, Edwards, Hawthorne, Emerson, Thoreau, Longfellow, and Melville. The place inspired him to accomplish his greatest literary feats.

One of Twain's most famous quips says that a literary classic is "a book which people praise and don't read." By that standard much of his own work has achieved classic status. Certainly, if anyone were to actually pay attention to the noisy multicultural debate over *The Adventures of Huckleberry Finn*, it would be obvious that those with the loudest opinions could never have actually read the book.

Be that as it may, it is likely that most people today know Twain from his sparkling, dead-on, humbug-piercing epigrams rather than his more extended writing. He once wrote, "The difference between the right word and the almost-right word is the difference between the lightning and the lightning-bug." And he knew that finding just the right word could be a mighty struggle. In a notebook page from the last decade of the nineteenth century, he left evidence of his great labor to breathe life into a new wisecrack:

"The man that invented the cuckoo clock is no more," he began.

Then come several attempts—all heavily scribbled over—in an effort to construct a suitable punch line:

"This is old news but good."

"As news, this is a little stale, but some news is better old than not at all."

"As news, this is a little old, but better late than never."

"As news, this is a little old, for it happened sixty-four years ago, but it is not always the newest news that is the best."

"It is old news, but there is nothing else the matter with it."

Finally, he must have concluded that no amount of polishing was going to make that particular material shine, for at the bottom of the page he wrote, resignedly, "It is more trouble to make a maxim than it is to do right."

But he did take the trouble, and most of the time he got it right—which is why we still quote Twain today, nearly a century after his death. In fact, to get a respectful hearing for just about any statement, a speaker need only preface it with the magic words, "As Mark Twain said . . . " Indeed, many a reader has taken on the project of filling a notebook with some of Twain's pithiest and wittiest quips—which is why the best of them are still quoted ad nauseum:

"It is agreed, in this country, that if a man can arrange his religion so that it perfectly satisfies his conscience, it is not incumbent on him to care whether the arrangement is satisfactory to anyone else or not."

"All you need is ignorance and confidence; then success is sure."

"It is better to keep your mouth shut and appear stupid than to open it and remove all doubt."

"When in doubt, tell the truth."

"By trying we can easily learn to endure adversity. Another man's, I mean."

"We all do no end of feeling, and we mistake it for thinking."

"Always do right. That will gratify some of the people, and astonish the rest."

"Grief can take care of itself, but to get the full value of a joy you must have somebody to divide it with."

"The political and commercial morals of the United States are not merely food for laughter, they are an entire banquet."

"It could probably be shown by facts and figures that there is no distinctly native American criminal class except Congress."

"The man who does not read good books has no advantage over the man who can't read them."

"If you invent two or three people and turn them loose in your manuscript, something is bound to happen to them—you can't help it; and then it will take you the rest of the book to get them out of the natural consequences of that occurrence, and so first thing you know, there's your book all finished up and never cost you an idea."

"It is by the goodness of God that in the West we have those three unspeakably precious things: freedom of speech, freedom of conscience, and the prudence never to practice either of them."

The bucolic environs that had spawned Tom Sawyer, Huck Finn, and all that witticism bristles with refinement and energy. The grandiloquent Twain house matches the grandiloquence of the man. The place is like a tonic of creative inspiration—in the same way that a visit to Winston Churchill's Chartwell, Teddy Roosevelt's Sagamore Hill, Hilaire Belloc's Kings Land, William Faulkner's Rowan Oak, William Butler Yeats's Thoor Ballylee, Vita Sackville-West's Sissinghurst, or Walter Scott's Abbotsford always is.

Indeed, such is the case with all literary associations.

A PRACTICUM ON JUSTICE

"None of us was 'lowed to see a book or try to learn. They say we git smarter than they was if we learn anything, but we slips around and gits hold of that Webster's old blue-back speller and we hides it till 'way in the night and then we lights a little pine torch, and studies that spelling book. We learn it too. I can read some now and write a little too."
JENNY PROCTOR (C. 1850–1910)

In any and every culture, it behooves those who are in control to keep those who are powerless in the dark, out of the loop—even, illiterate. All too many nineteenth-century American slave owners in both the North and South knew that. And contemporary societies whose purposes do not include genuine freedom of mind, heart, and spirit continue to practice varying sorts of limitation of access to the dissemination and accumulation of knowledge, understanding, and wisdom.

In writing about lovely visits to the homes of our own literary heroes and heroines, we must not neglect to at least mention a more disturbing literary tour. In your own locale, what areas are basically devoid of local bookshops, libraries, or even newsstands? In our own home in Tennessee, a struggle is going on over where the city's new much-needed library will be built. Will it be built on or near its current site, which is accessible to the poor in our community as well as the comparatively wealthy—in other words, those with their own means of available transportation—or will it move to the suburbs, where there is more land, more minivan parking, and more money? By the time this book is published, the council votes will most likely have been counted. But what about in your town?

In the community development primer he edited, *Restoring At-Risk Communities*, John Perkins writes about the kind of commitment it takes to bring hope to poor environments: "When the body of Christ is visibly present and living among the poor (relocation) and when we are loving our neighbor and our neighbor's family the way we love ourselves and our own family (reconciliation), the result is redistribution. It is not taking away from the rich and giving to the poor. Rather, it is when God's people with resources are living in the poor community and are a part of it, applying skills and resources to the problems of that community, thereby allowing a natural redistribution to occur. Redistribution is putting our lives, our skills, our education, and our resources to work to empower people in a community of need. Christian community development ministries find creative avenues to create jobs, schools, health centers, home ownership, and other enterprises of long-term development."

Imagine visiting a favorite writer's home, like Abbottsford, the beloved home of Sir Walter Scott set in the rolling hills of southern Scotland. The home is chock full of his collections, and his grandnieces informatively guide visitors through the rooms of books, armaments, and romantic impedimentia. The gardens surrounding the home are breathtaking, and for dessert, the back lawn rolls in a breathtaking vista into the River Tweed. The visitor knows Scott better for having toured his study, his living areas, and his beloved property.

Now imagine black holes, vacuums of places where such homes and literary meccas should stand, but none do. Nothingness. Imagine that you could do something about it. Think of the impact the writings of oppressed peoples have forever more. Anne Frank, for example, lives on through the journals of her short life. What voices need to learn to read and to write and to tell their stories?

There is much that we can all do to make sure that the great legacy of western civilization is passed on to the succeeding generations. The shelf life is anything but quiescent.

- Volunteer with a local literacy group.
- Spend one afternoon per week tutoring someone to read at a local school.
- For every ten books you buy yourself, donate one book to a school library in an impoverished area.

- Work to keep libraries accessible to poor areas in your locale.
- Give money toward school supplies for kids in low-income areas.
- Support the volunteers who go into low-income areas with gifts of encouragement, prayers, and support when they are weary of the battle.
- You are a taxpayer. Visit the schools your taxes subsidize and see how the money is spent and where the needs are. Listen to experts, but trust your own eyes.
- Care.

Literary Lists

*R*eaders are inveterate and unapologetic list makers. There
are lists of books that must be read. There are lists of books
that must be reread. There are lists of books that must be read
by others. There are lists of books that must be bought. There
are best-seller lists. There are best-of-the-best lists. There are
the indispensable book lists—those titles readers might profess
to be their preferred companions were they stranded on a
desert isle. It seems that list—making it simply goes with the
territory—is the natural accompaniment to the shelf life.

"Lists are the most necessary literary accessories of all."
Umberto Eco (1929–)

"Not only a person's catalog of books, but the very arrangement of them tells much about their character and disposi-
tion. An organized soul, for instance, might have only a
single book beside the bed. But a glutton sleeps with a vast
modern cityscape lurching mere inches away."
James Tallibrand (1852–1941)

"Make a list of books to be read and you have set the course
of a life well-spent."
Francis Bacon (1561–1626)

"A good catalog of the best books is a world of wisdom and adventure, virtue and valor, insight and experience all but for the asking. A young man who prefers other pursuits to the neglect of this goodly catalog may well be akin to the sloth; to be sure he is akin to the fool."

◆{ *Anthony Trollope (1815–1882)* }◆

"Pity the poor soul who finds entertainment in the buzzing distractions of this world, who finds amusement in the abandonment of the catalog of the canon of great books. His tiny world, his restricted scope, his narrow experience has robbed him of the fullness of life."

◆{ *Gustave Flaubert (1821–1880)* }◆

"What has become of that mystery of the printed word, of which Carlyle so movingly wrote? It has gone, it is to be feared, with those Memnonian mornings we sleep through with so determined snore, those ancient mysteries of night we forget beneath the mimic firmament of the music-hall. Only in the lamplit closet of the bookman, the fanatic of first and fine editions, is it remembered and revered. To him alone of an Americanized, pirate-edition reading world, the book remains the sacred thing it is."

Richard le Gallienne (1866–1901)

"Beware of popularity. Everybody's favorite book is nobody's."

Arthur Schopenhauer (1788–1860)

"There are a not few sadly mistaken moderns who actually believe that because a book is hard to read, it is hardly worth the effort. They have been robbed of their own indolence. Thus, the great lists of classics, the must-read catalogs, and the canons of the masterworks are closed universes to them. They have censored themselves. They have submitted to an intellectual apartheid of their own making. They have shackled themselves to the shallow, the petty, and the immediately accessible. They are to be pitied, above all else."

ᴏᶠ *Tristan Gylberd (1954–)* ᶠᴏ

"Oft, literary fame hath created something of nothing."

ᴏᶠ *Thomas Fuller (1608–1661)* ᶠᴏ

"In this world there are so few voices and so many echoes."

ᴏᶠ *Johann Goethe (1749–1834)* ᶠᴏ

"Normally I only care for a novel if the ending is good, and I quite agree that if the hero has to die he ought to die worthily and nobly, so that our sorrow at the tragedy shall be tempered with the joy and pride one always feels when a man does his duty well and bravely. There is quite enough sorrow and shame and suffering and baseness in real life, and there is no need for meeting it unnecessarily in fiction. As Police Commissioner it was my duty to deal with all kinds of squalid misery and hideous and unspeakable infamy, and I should have been worse than a coward if I had shrunk from doing what was necessary; but there would have been no use whatever in my reading novels detailing all this misery and squalor and crime, or at least in reading them as a steady thing. Now and then there is a powerful but sad story which really is interesting and which really does good; but normally the books which do good and the books which healthy people find interesting are those which are not in the least of the sugar-candy variety, but which, while portraying foulness and suffering when they must be portrayed, yet have a joyous as well as a noble side."

Theodore Roosevelt (1858–1919)

"I love reading another reader's list of favorites. Even when I find I do not share their tastes or predilections, I am provoked to compare, contrast, and contradict. It is a most healthy exercise, and one altogether fruitful."
T. S. Eliot (1888–1965)

"It is pretty clear that the majority, if they spoke without passion and were fully articulate, would not accuse us of liking the wrong books, but of making such a fuss about any books at all. We treat as a main ingredient in our well-being something which to them is marginal. Hence to say simply that they like one thing and we another is to leave out nearly the whole of the facts."
C. S. Lewis (1898–1963)

"If my life had been more full of calamity than it has been, I would live it all over again to have read the books I did in my youth. I have made a list of them, and it has made me wistful."
William Hazlitt (1778–1830)

"Never underestimate the power of books for children. Note this well: it was the literature we read before we attained sophistication, maturity, and adulthood that has done the most to mold our characters, frame our thoughts, and influence our lives. A catalog of such books might well afford us a better map of comprehension than all the machinations of psychology."

Richard Ogilvie (1902–1988)

"The books that charmed us in youth recall the delight ever afterwards; we are hardly persuaded there are any like them, any deserving equally of our affections. Fortunate if the best fall in our way during this susceptible and forming period of our lives."

A. Bronson Alcott (1799–1888)

"There ought to be space in every home for books, those books long before outgrown but which the sentimental reader simply cannot give away. They are the books that hold one's youth between their leaves, like flowers pressed on a half-forgotten summer's day. They are the stuff of legacy and ought to be passed from one generation to the next. There is no sadder sight that that of a once beloved tome, now orphaned at a thrift shop by heirs who have broken covenant with the past. They bespeak the selling of a birthright for a mess of pottage—or worse, a clutch of filthy lucre."

Justinian Kulvaci (1914–1991)

Catalogs and Thomas Jefferson

"Every household and every nation might do well to have on hand a full catalog of the world's greatest works—a library upon which the pillars of freedom might find their fullest and surest support."
THOMAS JEFFERSON (1743–1826)

During his term as vice president, Thomas Jefferson traveled to Baltimore on official business. He asked for a room in the city's best hotel. Not recognizing the great man—who always traveled quite modestly without a retinue of servants and dressed comfortably in soiled working clothes—the proprietor turned him away.

Soon after Jefferson's departure, the innkeeper was informed that he had just sent away the author of the Declaration of Independence and hero of the Revolutionary War. Horrified, he promptly dispatched a number of his employees to find the vice president and offer him as many rooms as he required.

Jefferson, who had already taken a room at another hotel, was not at all flattered or amused. He sent the man who found him back with the message, "Tell the innkeeper that I value his good intentions highly, but if he has no room for a dirty farmer, he shall have none for the vice president."

It was not merely the spirit of democratic solidarity or of judicial propriety that piqued Jefferson's ire in that situation. He had always prided himself as a man of the soil first and foremost. He was America's preeminent agrarian theorist. He was an avid gardener and a skilled botanist. His gardening journals have inspired generations of farmers and planters. And his agricultural innovations helped make American harvests the envy of the world.

He strongly believed that an attachment to the land was the chief mark of an advanced culture. He believed that the fate of a nation was ultimately decided by the attitude of that nation to its soil.

Of course, it is not as a humble agrarian that Jefferson is best remembered today. He was undoubtedly one of this nation's deepest thinkers—the drafter of the Declaration of Independence, founder of the University of Virginia, the third president, the impetus behind the Louisiana Purchase, and a true visionary who helped forge a unique national identity for his fledgling nation.

As a result of his varied interests and concerns, Jefferson placed as much emphasis on books and libraries as he did on farms and agriculture. He was constantly recommending books. He was as renowned for his reading lists and catalogs as he was for his hybrid tomatoes and broad leaf tobacco.

The Library of Congress was founded in 1800, making it the oldest federal cultural institution in the nation. Jefferson, who became president the following year, gleefully appointed the first two Librarians of Congress. As a man who often stated he could not live without books, he took a keen interest in the Library and its collection. Throughout both his administrations he personally recommended books for the growing catalog. Jefferson passionately held that the power of the intellect could and should shape a free and democratic society. Even after he returned to civilian life, he continued to offer his advice and counsel to the librarians in Washington.

In 1814 the invading British army swept into the city of Washington and burned the Capitol, including the entire Library of Congress. The following year Jefferson offered to sell his vast personal library, the largest and finest in the country, to the Congress to recommence its library. Congress gladly accepted his generous offer.

The catalog of books that Jefferson sold to Congress not only included more than double the number of volumes that had been in the destroyed Library of Congress, it expanded the scope of the Library far beyond the bounds of a legislative library devoted primarily to legal, economic, and historical works. Jefferson was a man of encyclopedic interests, and his library included works on architecture, the arts, science, literature, and geography. It contained books in French, Spanish, German, Latin, Greek, and one three-volume statistical work in Russian. He believed that the American legislature needed ideas and information on all subjects and in many languages in order to govern a democracy.

Anticipating the argument that his collection might be too comprehensive, he argued that there was "no subject to which a Member of Congress may not have occasion to refer."

The acquisition by Congress of Jefferson's library provided the base for the expansion of the Library's functions. The Jeffersonian concept of universality is the rational for the comprehensive collecting policies of today's Library of Congress. Jefferson's belief in the power of knowledge and the direct link between knowledge and democracy shaped the Library's philosophy of sharing its collections and services as widely as possible. Today, the Library of Congress is the largest library in the world, with more than 115 million items on approximately 530 miles of bookshelves. The collections include some 17 million books, 2 million recordings, 12 million photographs, 4 million maps, and 50 million manuscripts. Jefferson's vision has been realized in magnificent fashion.

Jefferson, however, was not simply interested in building up a vast catalog of classic works for the national library in Washington. He was also convinced that every able household ought to strive to collect a core canon of masterworks as a family legacy.

In response to a letter from his nephew, Robert Skipwith, Jefferson offered exhaustive counsel—including a huge list of necessary books—on how to build a respectable gentleman's library:

"I sat down with a design of executing your request to form a catalogue of books amounting to about £30 Sterling. But could by no means satisfy myself with any partial choice I could make. Thinking therefore it might be as agreeable to you, I have framed such a general collection as I think you would wish, and might in time find convenient, to procure. Out of this you will choose for yourself to the amount you mentioned for the present year, and may hereafter as shall be convenient proceed in completing the whole.

"A view of the second column in this catalogue would I suppose extort a smile from the face of gravity. Peace to its wisdom! Let me not awaken it. A little attention however to the nature of the human mind evinces that the entertainments of fiction are useful as well as pleasant. That they are pleasant when well written, every person feels who reads. But wherein is its utility, ask the reverend sage, big with the notion that nothing can be useful but the learned lumber of Greek and Roman reading with which his head is stored? I answer, every thing is useful which contributes to fix us in the principles and practice of virtue.

"When any signal act of charity or of gratitude, for instance, is presented either to our sight or imagination, we are deeply impressed with its beauty and feel a strong desire in ourselves of doing charitable and grateful acts also. On the contrary when we

see or read of any atrocious deed, we are disgusted with its defor-
mity and conceive an abhorrence of vice.

"Now every emotion of this kind is an exercise of our virtuous
dispositions; and dispositions of the mind, like limbs of the body,
acquire strength by exercise. But exercise produces habit; and in
the instance of which we speak, the exercise being of the moral
feelings, produces a habit of thinking and acting virtuously. We
never reflect whether the story we read be truth or fiction. If the
painting be lively, and a tolerable picture of nature, we are thrown
into a reverie, from which if we awaken it is the fault of the writer.
I appeal to every reader of feeling and sentiment whether the fictitious murder of Duncan by Macbeth in Shakespeare does not
excite in him as great horror of villainy, as the real one of Henry IV
by Ravaillac as related Davila? And whether the fidelity of Nelson,
and generosity of Blandford in Marmontel do not dilate his breast,
and elevate his sentiments as much as any similar incident which
real history can furnish? Does he not in fact feel himself a better
man while reading them, and privately covenant to copy the fair
example? We neither know nor care whether Lawrence Sterne
really went to France, whether he was there accosted by the poor
Franciscan, at first rebuked him unkindly, and then gave him a
peace offering; or whether the whole be not a fiction. In either case
we are equally sorrowful at the rebuke, and secretly resolve we will

never do so: we are pleased with the subsequent atonement, and view with emulation a soul candidly acknowledging its fault, and making a just reparation.

"Considering history as a moral exercise, her lessons would be too infrequent if confined to real life. Of those recorded by historians few incidents have been attended with such circumstances as to excite in any high degree this sympathetic emotion of virtue. We are therefore wisely framed to be as warmly interested for a fictitious as for a real personage. The spacious field of imagination is thus laid open to our use, and lessons may be formed to illustrate and carry home to the mind every moral rule of life. Thus a lively and lasting sense of filial duty is more effectually impressed on the mind of a son or daughter by reading King Lear, than by all the dry volumes of ethics and divinity that ever were written. This is my idea of well-written Romance, of Tragedy, Comedy, and Epic Poetry.

"If you are fond of speculation, the books under the head of Criticism, will afford you much pleasure. Of Politicks and Trade I have given you a few only of the best books, as you would probably choose to be not unacquainted with those commercial principles which bring wealth into our country, and the constitutional security we have for the enjoyment of that wealth."

"In Law I mention a few systematical books, as a knowledge of the minutiae of that science is not necessary for a private gentleman.

In Religion, History, Natural philosophy, I have followed the same plan in general.

"But whence the necessity of this collection? Come to the new Rowanty, from which you may reach your hand to a library formed on a more extensive plan. Separated from each other but a few paces, the possessions of each would be open to the other. A spring, centrically situated, might be the scene of every evening's joy. There we should talk over the lessons of the day, or lose the in Musick, Chess, or the merriments of our family companions. The heart thus lightened, our pillows would be soft, and health and long life would attend the happy scene."

Following a few personal notes, Jefferson concluded his counsel with an astonishingly varied list of books. To this day they evidence his wide learning and his abiding passion:

FINE ARTS
Observations on Gardening by Payne
Webb's *Essay on Painting*
Homer's *Odyssey*
Dryden's Translation of the *Virgil*
Milton's *Works*
Hoole's *Tasso*
Ossian with Blair's *Criticisms*
Telemachus by Dodsley
Capell's Shakespeare
Dryden's *Plays*
Addison's *Plays*
Otway's *Plays*
Rowe's *Works*
Thompson's *Works*
Young's *Works*
Home's *Plays*
Mallet's *Works*
Mason's Poetical *Works*
Terence's *Works*
Moliere's *Works*
Farquhar's *Works*
Steele's *Works*
Congreve's *Works*

Garric's *Dramatic Works*
Foote's *Dramatic Works*
Rousseau's *Eloisa*
Rousseau's *Emilius and Sophia*
Marmontel's *Moral Tales*
Gil Blas translated by Smollet
Don Quixote translated by Smollet
David Simple's *Works*
Smollet's *Roderic Random*
Smollet's *Peregrine Pickle*
Smollet's *Launcelot Graces*
Smollet's *Adventures of a Ginea*
Richardson's *Pamela*
Richardson's *Clarissa*
Richardson's *Grandison*
Richardson's *Fool of Quality*
Fielding's *Works*
Langhorne's *Constantia*
Langhorne's *Solyan and Almena*
Goldsmith's *Vicar of Wakefield*
Percy's *Runic Poems*
Percy's *Reliques of Ancient English Poetry*
Percy's *Han Kiou Chouan*

Percy's *Miscellaneous Chinese Pieces*
Chaucer's *Complete Works*
Spencer's *Complete Works*
Waller's *Poems*
Dodsley's *Collection of Poems*
Pearch's *Collection of Poems*
Gray's *Works*
Ogilvie's *Poems*
Prior's *Poems*
Gay's *Works*
Shenstone's *Works*
Dryden's *Works*
Pope's *Works* Collected by Warburton
Churchill's *Poems*
Swift's *Works*
Swift's *Literary Correspondence*
Addison and Steele's *Spectator*
Tatler
Guardian
Freeholder
Lord Lyttleton's *Persian Letters*

CRITICISM on the FINE ARTS
Lord Kaim's *Elements of Criticism*
Burke *On the Sublime and Beautiful*
Hogarth's *Analysis of Beauty*
Reid *On the Human Mind*
Smith's *Theory of Moral Sentiments*
Johnson's *Dictionary*
Capell's *Polusions*

POLITICKS
Montesquieu's *Spirit of Laws*
Locke on *Government*
Sidney on *Government*
Marmontel's *Belisarius*
Lord Bolingbroke's *Political Works*
Montesquieu's *Rise and Fall of the Roman Government*
Stuart's *Political Economy*
Petty's *Political Arithmetic*

METAPHYSIKS and PHILOSOPHY
Locke's *Conduct of the Mind in Search of Truth*
Xenophon's *Memoirs of Socrates*
Epictetus by Mrs. Carter
Antonius by Collins
Seneca by L'Estrange
Cicero's Offices by Guthrie
Cicero's *Tusculan Questions*
Lord Bolingbroke's *Philosophical Works*
Hume's *Essays*
Lord Kaim's *Natural Religion*
Philosophical Survey of Nature
Economy of Human Life
Sterne's *Sermons*
Sherlock *On Death*
Sherlock *On a Future State*

LAW
Lord Kaim's *Principles of Equity*
Blackstone's *Commentaries*
Cunningham's *Law Dictionary*

ANCIENT HISTORY
Bible
Rollin's *Ancient History*
Stanyan's *Graecian History*
Livy's *Works*
Sallust by Gordon
Tacitus by Gordon
Caesar by Bladen
Josephus's *History of the War*
Vertot's *Revolutions of Rome*
Plutarch's Lives Translated by Langhorne
Bayle's *Dictionary*
Jeffrey's *Historical & Chronological Chart*

MODERN HISTORY
Robertson's *History of Charles the Vth*
Bossuet's *History of France*
Davila by Farneworth
Hume's *History of England*
Clarendon's *History of the Rebellion*
Robertson's *History of Scotland*
Keith's *History of Virginia*
Stith's *History of Virginia*

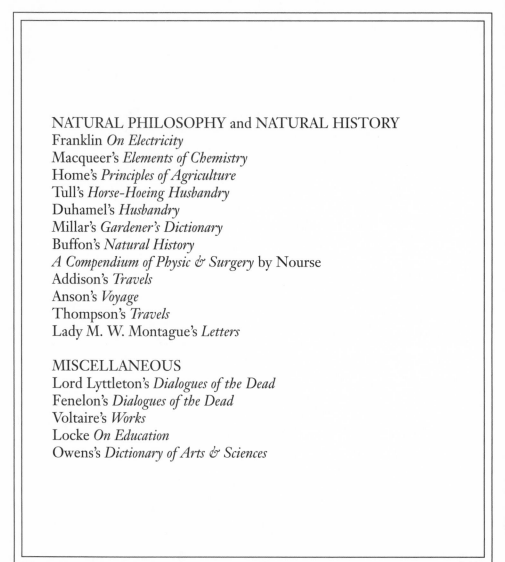

NATURAL PHILOSOPHY and NATURAL HISTORY
Franklin *On Electricity*
Macqueer's *Elements of Chemistry*
Home's *Principles of Agriculture*
Tull's *Horse-Hoeing Husbandry*
Duhamel's *Husbandry*
Millar's *Gardener's Dictionary*
Buffon's *Natural History*
A Compendium of Physic & Surgery by Nourse
Addison's *Travels*
Anson's *Voyage*
Thompson's *Travels*
Lady M. W. Montague's *Letters*

MISCELLANEOUS
Lord Lyttleton's *Dialogues of the Dead*
Fenelon's *Dialogues of the Dead*
Voltaire's *Works*
Locke *On Education*
Owens's *Dictionary of Arts & Sciences*

Fulwar Skipwith, the cousin of Robert Skipwith, quickly amended their uncle's list—his obvious intention was to balance out Jefferson's rather notable anti-Christian bias. He wrote, "Hearing of our esteemed uncle's recommendations for a gentleman's proper library, I could not but help to desire emendations upon several issues. Although his selections show the obvious felicity of mind from a lifetime of study, they also evidence peculiar biases, particularly in the questions of orthodox religion and the conduct of western Christendom. I therefore humbly offer these essential volumes for due consideration in your enterprise."

His list was not nearly as voluminous, though no less revealing than Jefferson's:

OVERVIEW CLASSICISM
Aristotle's *Rhetoric*
Aristotle's *Poetics*
Breatton's *Mythology*
Homer's *Illiad*
Plato's *Republic*

SURVEY PATRISTISM
Athanasius's *On the Incarnation*
Augustine's *Confessions*
Augustine's *The City of God*
Malory's *Le Mort d'Arthur*
Joinville's *Chronicles of the Crusades*
Villehardouin's *Chronicles of the Crusades*

RENAISSANCE PRACTICUM
Dante's *Inferno*
Erasmus's *In Praise of Folly*
Machiavelli's *Prince*
Vasari's *Lives of the Artists*

REFORMATION THEOLOGY
Bunyan's P*ilgrim's Progress*
Calvin's *Institutes*
Knox's *History of the Reformation in Scotland*
Luther's *Bondage of the Will*
Westminster Confession of Faith

MODERN SOCIAL CRITICISM
Johnson's *Lives of the Poets*
Johnson's *Rasselas*
More's *Utopia*
Rousseau's *The Social Contact*
Spenser's *The Fairie Queen*
Burke's *Reflections on the Revolution in France*
Cromwell's *Speeches*

A Practicum on Verse

"To hear the strains of the great eighth century Celtic hymn, 'Be Thou My Vision,' even in its modern translation by Byrne and Hull, is to comprehend the full magnificence, all at once, of the incredible legacy of English verse. Hymnology, though sorely neglected, is part and parcel of our most glorious inheritance."
ARTHUR QUILLER-COUCH (1863-1944)

"Be Thou my Vision, O Lord of my heart;
Nought be all else to me, save that Thou art—
Thou my best thought, by day or by night,
Waking or sleeping, Thy presence my light.

"Be Thou my Wisdom, and Thou my true Word;
I ever with Thee and Thou with me, Lord;
Thou my great Father, and I Thy true son,
Thou in me dwelling, and I with Thee one.

"Riches I heed not, nor man's empty praise,
Thou mine inheritance, now and always;
Thou and Thou only, first in my heart,
High King of heaven, my treasure Thou art.

"High King of heaven, my victory won,
May I reach heaven's joys, O bright heaven's Sun!
Heart of my own heart, whatever befall,
Still be my Vision, O Ruler of all."
Mary Elizabeth Byrne (1880–1931)
and Eleanor Henrietta Hull (1860–1935)

When we think of reading poetry, one classification frequently overlooked is that of the wonderful hymns of the ages. There are hymns for meditation upon every state of the heart. Hymns divide the seasons of the year, and they speak eloquently for us when we can't find words of our own in times of celebration, grief, worship, repentance, or introspection. When forgiveness is only an act of will with no concurrent feeling, hymns remind us of our own forgiveness and instruct our emotions in the way they should go. When crying out for a wayward child, over an empty womb, or over financial duress, hymns express the guttural sensations of our very souls. Perhaps this is why the book of Psalms in the Bible, composed in great part of the hymns of the very human King David, is the most common devotional book in the sacred text. It is poetry for the soul, full of expressions of fear, anger, euphoria, self-congratulation, fealty and worship, heroic tales, and awe over creation's beauty. Incorporate hymns into your own reading of poetry and be the richer for it as you discover and rediscover kindred spirits in the path of life.

- Obtain a copy of the Psalms in meter. For a long time included in the back of service books in many churches, metrical Psalms are Psalms reworded into the common meter. You will be able to sing them to familiar tunes.
- Take a hymnbook outside early in the morning and sing through the pages of familiar old hymns in preparation for the upcoming day.
- Keep a hymnal at bedside and prepare your mind and spirit for rest by meditating over one hymn each evening.
- Find a favorite Psalm and rewrite it as a hymn in your own journal.
- Collect old hymnbooks from diverse traditions in used bookstores. They are not expensive, and what a valuable collection it will be to you!
- Look up the hymn writer of a favorite hymn in the back of the hymnal and trace his or her growth in other hymns included in your hymn collection.
- Collect CD's of instrumental versions of your favorite hymns.
- The very best anthologies of poetry ever assembled in any

language are arguably *The Oxford Book of English Verse* and *The Oxford Book of English Ballads*, both edited by Arthur Quiller-Couch (1863–1944). *Q*, as he was best known, was a brilliant novelist, poet, essayist, and university lecturer in his own right. What makes his anthologies so delightful, is not only their breadth and depth and width, their undeniable scholarship, and their immediate accessibility, but their deep appreciation for hymnology as well. By all means, find, keep, and enjoy *Q*'s greatest legacy.

Literary Bests

*I*s it possible to identify modern literary classics? Are we actually able to judge contemporary works apart from the judgments of time? Some would argue that the evidence for greatness may be detected even in the closest proximity while others assert that such myopia eliminates any hope of objectivity. Though a good case may be made for either side of that debate, there is no denying that critics will make the attempt regardless. And so they do.

"All books are divisible into two classes, the books of the hour, and the books of all time. Mark this distinction—it is not one of quality only. It is not merely the bad book that does not last, and the good one that does. It is a distinction of species. There are good books for the hour, and good books for all time; bad books for the hour, and bad ones for all time."

John Ruskin (1819–1900)

"The best effect of any book is that it excited the reader to self activity."

Thomas Carlyle (1795–1881)

"Literary experience heals the wound, without undermining the privilege, of individuality. Here, as in worship, in love, in moral action, and in knowing, I transcend myself; and am never more myself than when I do."

C. S. Lewis (1898–1963)

"Though we don't have much to show for it, we Americans are enthusiasts for education. The problem is that we engage in the eminently dubious process of what is barbarously known as standardization. As a result, we lower our ideals and we smear our philosophy by playing the sedulous ape to popular uniformitarian educational fads and fashions. The only solution is to restore the basic educational ideals and principles that provoked Christendom's great flowering of culture in the first place: a strident emphasis on serious and diverse reading, the use of classical methodologies, and all this integrated into the gracious environs of Christian family life."

Leo Brennan (1901–1977)

"In life, as in literature, our admiration for mere cleverness has a touch of contempt in it, and is very unlike the respect paid to character."

George Henry Lewes (1817–1878)

"What I like in a good author is not what he says, but what he whispers."
Logan Pearsall Smith (1865–1946)

"Desire of knowledge, like the thirst of riches, increases ever with the acquisition of it. Reading—reading substantively, artfully, and thoughtfully—only aggravates the effect."
Laurence Sterne (1713–1768)

"Learning hath gained most by those books by which the printers have lost."
Thomas Fuller (1608–1661)

"About the most originality that any writer can hope to achieve honestly is to steal with good judgment."
⊶ Josh Billings (1818–1885) ⊷

"It is a terrible tragedy to be ignorant. It is more tragic still to be ignorant of your ignorance."
⊶ St. Jerome (c. 342–420) ⊷

"If one author steals from another, it's plagiarism; but if he steals from many, it's research."
⊶ Wilson Mizner (1876–1933) ⊷

"Every man is a borrower and a mimic; life is theatrical and literature a quotation."

Ralph Waldo Emerson (1803–1882)

"The formula two and two makes five is not without its attractions. It is the very formula for the creative arts in literature."

Fedor Dostoevsky (1821–1881)

"I would just as soon write free verse as play tennis with the net down."

Robert Frost (1874–1963)

"Most colleges hate geniuses, just as most convents hate saints and most publishers hate poets."
        ∞ *Ralph Waldo Emerson (1803–1882)* ∞

"Mediocrity knows nothing higher than itself, but talent instantly recognizes genius."
        ∞ *Arthur Conan Doyle (1859–1930)* ∞

"Great ideas have a very short shelf life."
        ∞ *John Shanahan (1939–)* ∞

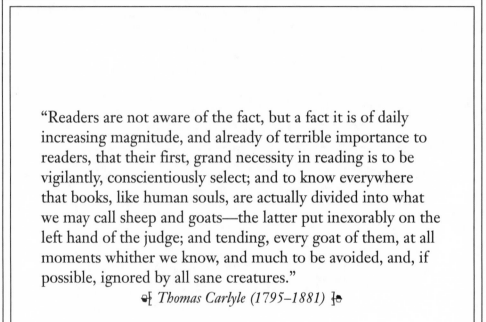

"Readers are not aware of the fact, but a fact it is of daily increasing magnitude, and already of terrible importance to readers, that their first, grand necessity in reading is to be vigilantly, conscientiously select; and to know everywhere that books, like human souls, are actually divided into what we may call sheep and goats—the latter put inexorably on the left hand of the judge; and tending, every goat of them, at all moments whither we know, and much to be avoided, and, if possible, ignored by all sane creatures."

Thomas Carlyle (1795–1881)

"For ne'er
Was flattery lost on a poet's ear
A simple race! They waste their toil
For the vain tribute of a smile."

Walter Scott (1771–1832)

"There is no misanthropic thief like a bad book; no philan-thropic benefactor like a good one."

ᙏ *Tristan Gylberd (1954–)* ᙎ

"Immature poets imitate; mature poets steal."

ᙏ *T. S. Eliot (1888–1965)* ᙎ

"The best part of every author is in general to be found in his book."

ᙏ *Samuel Johnson (1709–1784)* ᙎ

"The chief glory of every people arises from its authors."

ᙏ *Samuel Johnson (1709–1784)* ᙎ

"Never read a book through merely because you have
begun it."

John Witherspoon (1723–1794)

"Not marble, nor the gilded monuments
Of princes, shall outlive this powerful rhyme."

William Shakespeare (c. 1564–1616)

"Reading is to the mind what exercise is to the body. As by
the one, health is preserved, strengthened, and invigorated;
by the other, virtue—which is the health of the mind—is
kept alive, cherished, and confirmed."

Joseph Addison (1672–1719)

"Some books are meant to be tasted, others to be swallowed, and some few to be chewed and digested; that is, some books are to be read only in parts; others to be read but not curiously; and some few to be read wholly, and with diligence and attention."

Francis Bacon (1561–1626)

"I would have everybody able to read and write and cipher; indeed, I don't think a man can know too much; but mark you, the knowing of these things is not education; and there are millions of your reading and writing people who are as ignorant as neighbor Norton's calf."

Charles Spurgeon (1834–1892)

THE MODERN LIBRARY NONFICTION LIST

In preparation for the advent of the twenty-first century, numerous retrospective studies have attempted to put the twentieth century in some kind of perspective. By almost any measure, it has been a century of disasters and disappointments—the most brutal evidence of man's inhumanity to man in the whole of history has been perpetrated during the last hundred years. Alas, while our scientific achievements have been great, our cultural milestones have been few and far between. The publishers of the Modern Library—a series of twentieth-century classics—attempted, early in 1999 to rate the best books of our time. Their list betrays some of the biases that have made this a rather dismal epoch—it is ideological, rootless, and wildly existential. Besides this list of their top twenty-five, other books that drew their attention included: *The Souls of Black Folk*, W. E. B. Du Bois; *A Study of History*, Arnold J. Toynbee; *The Autobiography of Malcolm X*, Alex Haley and Malcolm X; *The Right Stuff*, Tom Wolfe; *Eminent Victorians*, Lytton Strachey; *The Open Society and Its Enemies*, Karl Popper; *A Preface to Morals*, Walter Lippmann; and *In Cold Blood*, Truman Capote.

1. *The Education of Henry Adams*, Henry Adams
2. *The Varieties of Religious Experience*, William James
3. *Up from Slavery*, Booker T. Washington
4. *A Room of One's Own*, Virginia Woolf
5. *Silent Spring*, Rachel Carson
6. *Selected Essays*, T. S. Eliot
7. *The Double Helix*, James D. Watson
8. *Speak, Memory*, Vladimir Nabokov
9. *The American Language*, H. L. Mencken
10. *The General Theory of Employment, Interest, and Money*, John Maynard Keynes
11. *The Lives of a Cell*, Lewis Thomas
12. *The Frontier in American History*, Frederick Jackson Turner
13. *Black Boy*, Richard Wright
14. *Aspects of the Novel*, E. M. Forster
15. *The Civil War*, Shelby Foote
16. *The Guns of August*, Barbara Tuchman
17. *The Proper Study of Mankind*, Isaiah Berlin
18. *The Nature and Destiny of Man*, Reinhold Niebuhr
19. *Notes of a Native Son*, James Baldwin
20. *The Autobiography of Alice B. Toklas*, Gertrude Stein
21. *The Elements of Style*, William Strunk and E. B. White
22. *An American Dilemma*, Gunnar Myrdal
23. *Principia Mathematica*, Alfred North Whitehead and Bertrand Russell
24. *The Mismeasure of Man*, Stephen Jay Gould
25. *The Mirror and the Lamp*, Meyer Howard Abrams

THE MODERN LIBRARY FICTION LIST

The Modern Library nonfiction list was naturally controversial. But its fiction list created an even greater furor. And for good reason. It evidences the proclivity of modern New York publishers to focus on the sensational rather than the substantive, the fascinating rather than the enduring, the shocking rather than the affirming, and the fashionable rather than the true, good, and beautiful. Other books that made the grade on this list included: *The Ambassadors*, Henry James; *Tender Is the Night*, F. Scott Fitzgerald; *Lord of the Flies*, William Golding; *Deliverance*, James Dickey; *Women in Love*, D. H. Lawrence; *Tropic of Cancer*, Henry Miller; *The Naked and the Dead*, Norman Mailer; *Portnoy's Complaint*, Philip Roth; *On the Road*, Jack Kerouac; *The Maltese Falcon*, Dashiell Hammett; *The Catcher in the Rye*, J. D. Salinger; *Lord Jim*, Joseph Conrad; *Ragtime*, E. L. Doctorow; *Midnight's Children*, Salman Rushdie; *The Magus*, John Fowles; and *Sophie's Choice*, William Styron.

1. *Ulysses*, James Joyce
2. *The Great Gatsby*, F. Scott Fitzgerald
3. *A Portrait of the Artist as a Young Man*, James Joyce
4. *Lolita*, Vladimir Nabokov
5. *Brave New World*, Aldous Huxley
6. *The Sound and the Fury*, William Faulkner
7. *Catch-22*, Joseph Heller
8. *Darkness at Noon*, Arthur Koestler
9. *Sons and Lovers*, D. H. Lawrence
10. *The Grapes of Wrath*, John Steinbeck
11. *Under the Volcano*, Malcolm Lowry
12. *The Way of All Flesh*, Samuel Butler
13. *1984*, George Orwell
14. *I, Claudius*, Robert Graves
15. *To the Lighthouse*, Virginia Woolf
16. *An American Tragedy*, Theodore Dreiser
17. *The Heart Is a Lonely Hunter*, Carson McCullers
18. *Slaughterhouse-Five*, Kurt Vonnegut
19. *Invisible Man*, Ralph Ellison
20. *Native Son*, Richard Wright
21. *Henderson the Rain King*, Saul Bellow
22. *Appointment in Samarra*, John O'Hara
23. *U.S.A.*, John Dos Passos
24. *Winesburg, Ohio*, Sherwood Anderson
25. *A Passage to India*, E. M. Forster

THE MODERN LIBRARY READERS LIST

Partisans of Ayn Rand, L. Ron Hubbard, J. R. R. Tolkien, Robert Heinlein, and other popular twentieth-century authors who were excluded from the Modern Library lists flooded the offices of Random House with a bevy of protests. As a result, the editors were forced to create an alternative list. Other books that readers affirmed as the best of this century include: *A Prayer for Owen Meany*, John Irving; *The Stand*, Stephen King; *Beloved*, Toni Morrison; *At the Mountains of Madness*, H. P. Lovecraft; *One Lonely Night*, Mickey Spillane; *A Clockwork Orange*, Anthony Burgess; *Ender's Game*, Orson Scott Card; *The Sun Also Rises*, Ernest Hemingway; *Zen and the Art of Motorcycle Maintenance*, Robert Pirsig; *Fahrenheit 451*, Ray Bradbury; *One Flew Over the Cuckoo's Nest*, Ken Kesey; *Illusions*, Richard Bach; and *The Satanic Verses*, Salman Rushdie.

1. *Atlas Shrugged*, Ayn Rand
2. *The Fountainhead*, Ayn Rand
3. *Battlefield Earth*, L. Ron Hubbard
4. *The Lord of the Rings*, J. R. R. Tolkien
5. *To Kill a Mockingbird*, Harper Lee
6. *1984*, George Orwell
7. *Anthem*, Ayn Rand
8. *We the Living*, Ayn Rand
9. *Mission Earth*, L. Ron Hubbard
10. *Fear*, L. Ron Hubbard
11. *Ulysses*, James Joyce
12. *Catch-22*, Joseph Heller
13. *The Great Gatsby*, F. Scott Fitzgerald
14. *Dune*, Frank Herbert
15. *The Moon Is a Harsh Mistress*, Robert Heinlein
16. *Stranger in a Strange Land*, Robert Heinlein
17. *A Town Like Alice*, Nevil Shute
18. *Brave New World*, Aldous Huxley
19. *The Catcher in the Rye*, J. D. Salinger
20. *Animal Farm*, George Orwell
21. *Gravity's Rainbow*, Thomas Pynchon
22. *The Grapes of Wrath*, John Steinbeck
23. *Slaughterhouse Five*, Kurt Vonnegut
24. *Gone With the Wind*, Margaret Mitchell
25. *Lord of the Flies*, William Golding

*T*HE *NATIONAL REVIEW* NONFICTION LIST

It was inevitable that others would weigh in on the issue of which books ought to be recognized as the best of the century. *The National Review*, long the lone voice of political and economic conservatism in American journalism issued a predictably right-leaning list. While it tends to be ideologically over-weighted, it provides a useful balance to the inhuman humanism of the Modern Library lists. Other books mentioned by *National Review* editors included: *The Quest for Community*, Robert Nisbet; *The Closing of the American Mind*, Allan Bloom; *Ethnic America*, Thomas Sowell; *Three Case Histories*, Sigmund Freud; *The Elements of Style*, William Strunk and E. B. White; *R. E. Lee*, Douglas Southall Freeman; *Bureaucracy*, Ludwig Von Mises; *The Good Society*, Walter Lippmann; *Silent Spring*, Rachel Carson; *Mont-Saint-Michel and Chartres*, Henry Adams; *The Conservative Mind*, Russell Kirk; *Wealth and Poverty*, George Gilder; *The Electric Kool Aid Acid Test*, Tom Wolfe; *Darwin's Black Box*, Michael J. Behe; *To the Finland Station*, Edmund Wilson; *The Last Lion*, William Manchester; and *The Starr Report*, Kenneth W. Starr.

1. *The Second World War,* Winston S. Churchill
2. *The Gulag Archipelago,* Aleksandr Solzhenitsyn
3. *Homage to Catalonia,* George Orwell
4. *The Road to Serfdom,* F. A. von Hayek
5. *Collected Essays,* George Orwell
6. *The Open Society and Its Enemies,* Karl Popper
7. *The Abolition of Man,* C. S. Lewis
8. *Revolt of the Masses,* José Ortega y Gasset
9. *The Constitution of Liberty,* F. A. von Hayek
10. *Capitalism and Freedom,* Milton Friedman
11. *Modern Times,* Paul Johnson
12. *Rationalism in Politics,* Michael Oakeshott
13. *Capitalism, Socialism, and Democracy,* Joseph A. Schumpeter
14. *Economy and Society,* Max Weber
15. *The Origins of Totalitarianism,* Hannah Arendt
16. *Black Lamb and Grey Falcon,* Rebecca West
17. *Sociobiology,* Edward O. Wilson
18. *Centissimus Annus,* Pope John Paul II
19. *The Pursuit of the Millennium,* Norman Cohn
20. *The Diary of a Young Girl,* Anne Frank
21. *The Great Terror,* Robert Conquest
22. *Chronicles of Wasted Time,* Malcolm Muggeridge
23. *Relativity,* Albert Einstein
24. *Witness,* Whittaker Chambers
25. *The Structure of Scientific Revolutions,* Thomas S. Kuhn

THE *WORLD* MAGAZINE LIST

The editors of the Christian news magazine *World* offered their own list. While the Modern Library lists is biased by liberal humanism and *The National Review* list is biased by conservative libertarianism, the *World* list is biased by religious right traditionalism—admittedly a far preferable thing to the other two alternatives. Other books mentioned on their list included: *Darkness at Noon*, Arthur Koestler; *Killer Angels*, Michael Shaara; *Jesus Rediscovered*, Malcolm Muggeridge; *The Diary of a Young Girl*, Anne Frank; *The Hiding Place*, Corrie Ten Boom; *The Road to Serfdom*, F. A. Hayek; *The God That Failed*, Richard Crossman; *The Origins of Totalitarianism*, Hannah Arendt; *The Humiliation of the Word*, Jacques Ellul; *A Study of History*, Arnold J. Toynbee; *The Structure of Scientific Revolution*, Thomas Kuhn; *The Closing of the American Mind*, Allan Bloom; *The Education of Henry Adams*, Henry Adams; and *The Conservative Mind*, Russell Kirk.

1. *Mere Christianity*, C. S. Lewis,
2. *The Collected Poems*, T. S. Eliot
3. *Orthodoxy*, G. K. Chesterton
4. *The God Who Is There*, Francis Schaeffer
5. *The Fundamentals*, J. Gresham Machen et al.
6. *The Gulag Archipelago*, Alexandr Solzhenitsyn
7. *Witness*, Whittaker Chambers
8. *Christianity and Liberalism*, J. Gresham Machen
9. *The Defense of the Faith*, Cornelius Van Til
10. *The Lord of the Rings*, J. R. R. Tolkien
11. *Up from Slavery*, Booker T. Washington
12. *Battle for the Bible*, Harold Lindsell
13. *Spiritual Depression*, D. Martyn Lloyd-Jones
14. *The Quest for Holiness*, Adolf Koeberle
15. *The Pursuit of God*, A. W. Tozier
16. *The Cost of Discipleship*, Dietrich Bonhoeffer
17. *The Mind of the Maker*, Dorothy Sayers
18. *Modern Art and the Death of a Culture*, Hans Rookmaaker
19. *The Violent Bear It Away*, Flannery O'Connor
20. *The Power and the Glory*, Graham Greene
21. *1984*, George Orwell
22. *Brave New World*, Aldous Huxley
23. *The Descent into Hell*, Charles Williams
24. *Lord of the Flies*, William Golding
25. *Lost in the Cosmos*, Walker Percy

THE SOUTHERN LITERATURE LIST

Under the editorship of Donald Davidson, one of the Southern Agrarians at Vanderbilt University, the daily Nashville newspaper, the *Tennessean*, became a beacon light of literary criticism throughout the middle of the century. Following Davidson's death two decades ago, the paper has suffered a steady and precipitous decline—alas, it is now owned by the scion of lowest-common-denominator American liberal journalism, Gannett. Nevertheless, from time to time the paper does hearken back to its roots as evidenced by this list. Notice, though, that all the works of William Faulkner are excluded from the list. This was not due to an egregious oversight. In fact, the editors so highly esteem the work of Faulkner that they felt it actually transcended the list. They wrote, "To define, discuss, or write about Southern literature is, in one way or another, to engage William Faulkner." Thus, all of the Faulkner canon stands front and center, perhaps even over and above the other books on this list: *The Sound and the Fury*; *As I Lay Dying*; *Light in August*; *Absalom, Absalom*; *Go Down Moses*; *The Unvanquished*; *Sanctuary*; and *The Collected Stories*.

1. *The Golden Apples*, Eudora Welty
2. *Lie Down in Darkness*, William Styron
3. *The Moviegoer*, Walker Percy
4. *Wise Blood*, Flannery O'Connor
5. *All the King's Men*, Robert Penn Warren
6. *The Optimist's Daughter*, Eudora Welty
7. *The Confessions of Nat Turner*, William Styron
8. *The Heart Is a Lonely Hunter*, Carson McCullers
9. *A Death in the Family*, James Agee
10. *Native Son*, Richard Wright
11. *Other Voices, Other Rooms*, Truman Capote
12. *Look Homeward Angel*, Thomas Wolfe
13. *The Violent Bear It Away*, Flannery O'Connor
14. *The Second Coming*, Walker Percy
15. *Their Eyes Were Watching God*, Zora Hurston
16. *To Kill a Mockingbird*, Harper Lee
17. *A Lesson Before Dying*, Ernest Gaines
18. *Blood Meridian*, Cormac McCarthy
19. *A Confederacy of Dunces*, John Kennedy Toole
20. *The Surface of the Earth*, Reynolds Price
21. *Deliverance*, James Dickey
22. *The Old Forest and Other Stories*, Peter Taylor
23. *The Yearling*, Marjorie Rawlings
24. *The Wold Birds*, Wendell Berry
25. *A Good Man Is Hard to Find*, Flannery O'Connor

THE BANNOCKBURN COLLEGE NONFICTION LIST

We couldn't help ourselves: we simply had to get in our two cents' worth. Compiling a list of the twenty-five best nonfiction works of the twentieth century is harder than it might appear at first glance—at least partly because most of the really good books written in this century are barely up to the standards of mediocre books written in earlier centuries. But, of course, in accord with God's good providence, there have been a number of happy literary aberrations. Almost any of the books by G. K. Chesterton, Abraham, Kuyper, Hilaire Belloc, C. S. Lewis, Dorothy Sayers, Niall Ferguson, Arthur Quiller-Couch, or Paul Johnson might have made the list—but we had to start and stop somewhere.

1. *Orthodoxy*, G. K. Chesterton
2. *The Stone Lectures*, Abraham Kuyper
3. *Knowing God*, J. I. Packer
4. *Mont St. Michel and Chartres*, Henry Adams
5. *The Servile State*, Hilaire Belloc
6. *Up from Slavery*, Booker T. Washington
7. *The Birth of the Modern*, Paul Johnson
8. *Hero Tales of American History*, Theodore Roosevelt and Henry Cabot Lodge
9. *The Gathering Storm*, Winston Churchill
10. *A World Torn Apart*, Aleksandr Solzhenitsyn
11. *Home*, Witold Rybczynski
12. *A Texan Looks at Lyndon*, J. Evetts Haley
13. *How the Other Half Lives*, Jacob Riis
14. *My Utmost for His Highest*, Oswald Chambers
15. *I'll Take My Stand*, Donald Davidson, et al.
16. *George Whitefield*, Arnold Dallimore
17. *84 Charing Cross Road*, Helene Hanff
18. *The Calvinistic Concept of Culture*, Henry Van Til
19. *A Wake for the Living*, Andrew Lytle
20. *A Christian Manifesto*, Francis Schaeffer
21. *Where Nights Are Longest*, Colin Thubron
22. *Amusing Ourselves to Death*, Neil Postman
23. *Civil Rights*, Thomas Sowell
24. *Essays and Criticisms*, Dorothy Sayers
25. *Ideas Have Consequences*, Richard M. Weaver

THE BANNOCKBURN COLLEGE FICTION AND VERSE LIST

From this close distance, it is very difficult to tell which novels from our time will continue to have relevance in the days to come. Like any list, this one is subjective and reflects our peculiar interests, biases, and concerns. At the same time it is rather wide ranging. Many of the writers included on this list could have had any number of their works listed. And writers such as Robert Penn Warren, Larry Woiwode, T. H. White, Rudyard Kipling, Wendell Berry, Peter Ackroyd, Eudora Welty, Ellis Peters, James Blaylock, Walter Miller, Allen Tate, John Crowe Ransom, and Flannery O'Connor probably should have been included somewhere but there just wasn't room.

1. *Oxford Book of English Verse*, Arthur Quiller-Couch
2. *The Lord of the Rings*, J. R. R. Tolkien
3. *The Father Brown Stories*, G. K. Chesterton
4. *Witch Wood*, John Buchan
5. *The Four Quartets*, T. S. Eliot
6. *The Space Trilogy*, C. S. Lewis
7. *A Day in the Life of Ivan Denisovich*, Aleksandr Solzhenitsyn
8. *The Four Men*, Hilaire Belloc
9. *Penhally*, Caroline Gordon
10. *Collected Stories*, William Faulkner
11. *The Wonderful Wizard of Oz*, L. Frank Baum
12. *Charlotte's Web*, E. B. White
13. *Scaramouche*, Rafael Sabatini
14. *The Name of the Rose*, Umberto Eco
15. *Kristen Lavransdatter*, Sigrid Undset
16. *Love in the Ruins*, Walker Percy
17. *The Velvet Horn*, Andrew Lytle
18. *The Footsteps at the Lock*, Ronald Knox
19. *The Weekend Wodehouse*, P. G. Wodehouse
20. *Falling*, Colin Thubron
21. *Little House on the Prairie*, Laura Ingalls Wilder
22. *The Anubis Gates*, Tim Powers
23. *Song of the Lark*, Willa Cather
24. *Possession*, A. S. Byatt
25. *At Home in Mitford*, Jan Karon

A PRACTICUM ON OUTSIDE READING

*"When I am with Miriam in the kitchen, she speaks of the past. I listen,
trying to imagine the world from which her cuisine came. I know gefilte
fish tastes different when you chop it by hand; I'm sure the flavor is
altered when you have lived Miriam's life: I met my husband in Chestochowa. I was beat up in Chestochowa. They wanted to take my father
away. I held on to him—like this, and I wouldn't let them take him.
They were beating me and beating me but I wouldn't let go, and they
didn't take my father. I didn't even feel it that time, the pain, I was so
excited. I could only think about keeping my father with me. But when I
got back to the barracks my whole neck and back were black. Afterward,
it hurt me. It got worse every year. Now, it's something terrible, I can't
do what I used to anymore. I can't take the vacuum cleaner even. Jacob
is doing the vacuuming for me. After ten minutes my back is hurting so
much I have to stop. It has a name, what's wrong with me. The German
doctor wrote it. I forget what it is called. Later they took my father
away, to Buchenwald. He was very sick and hungry. He died a day
before the American army came. 'Eat a piece of cake, mamele. Nem a
cookie, oytser sheyner. What shall I bake for you next week?' "*

ELIZABETH ERLICH (1933–)

Reading outside the "walls" of our lives—our own circumstances and culture, for instance—enlarges those walls. *Miriam's Kitchen*, by Elizabeth Erlich, is a great example. After the historical information about the holocaust has been learned, concentration camps visited, and horrible photographs assimilated into our body of learning, we still have to read about it sometimes to remember how evil we ourselves could be if we don't remember and guard our own hearts. Holocausts happen in Rwanda; why doesn't anyone do anything about them there? China systematically martyrs Christians; who takes their part? And little children are shot at in Jewish daycare centers because of ignorant revisionism in our own literate nation.

We've written elsewhere about how travel expands our mental boundaries. Within the four walls of our own homes, we can dispute, disagree with, wrestle over, laugh with, and finally find some commonality with human beings who would otherwise never cross our own paths. True, we both lean toward European writers who are characterized in our day as romantics. But in our own reading, we try not to limit ourselves to our own predilections. That would be no different than eating our favorite meal every single day of our lives, or experiencing the same season forever (which actually occurred when we lived in south Florida, but we won't go into that).

We love making new friends. Some of our friends are writers, and some are in corporate careers. Some are in full-time ministry, some are musicians. Surely our worlds would be suffocatingly small if all our friends were alike. Long ago, we realized that if we became friends with only those on whom we agreed on every point, not only would we be friendless, but also unmarried! We like best those with their own opinions and interests, who sometimes surge ahead of sensibilities against all odds to continue their study, or calling, or crusade. These people make for interesting and quite wonderful friends. We respect them for their honor and their heart.

So it is with reading. Through expanding our literary palette a little beyond our comfort zones, we find lifelong friends whom we will never have a chance to meet in this lifetime. From Jane Austen to Plato, from Jeremy Rifkin to Elizabeth Prentiss, Thomas Chalmers, Rumer Godden, Susan Hunt, Witold Rybczynski to Augustine of Hippo, if the writer will refrain from the profane in ignorant striving for cheap notoriety and acclaim and if they can tell a good story, we're hooked.

• Read outside your own interests. Once in a blue moon, pick up a book on astronomy, or Polish history, or theology a little different from your own. Wrestle with it.

- Find something in your interest areas by someone you would never ever run across in your daily life.
- Read outside your own century. The best of the best from our own time certainly should not be ignored. But all too often we are walled in by the bias of our own time. Read heavily well outside our time as well as within it.
- Subscribe to at least one magazine or newspaper from a foreign country, just to expand your world-view a bit. Pay attention to what others think of Americans and why.
- Be familiar with the rhetoric of those with whom you heartily disagree. Often their victories are born in areas where your camp has refused to address important issues.
- Join a reading circle composed of those outside your circle of friends. You don't have to contribute much if you don't want, just listen to their stories and what made them who they are today. They may not become your bosom buddies, but new reading buddies! It's okay to have differing levels of friendship.
- Just do it! Read!